A Must See**!**

A Must See!

★ *BRILLIANT* ★
BROADWAY ARTWORK

BY STEVEN SUSKIN

CHRONICLE BOOKS
SAN FRANCISCO

For!

Helen, Johanna, and **Charlie**

The artwork contained in this book is drawn mostly from the
collections of Max A. Woodward, Paul Newman, Richard Kidwell,
and a collector who wishes to remain anonymous.
To each of them, I am truly grateful and deeply indebted.
I would also like to thank Alan E. Rapp and Jodi Davis of Chronicle Books,
Adrienne Wiley of becker&mayer*!*, and designer Brett MacFadden
for their suggestions, enhancements, and support.

Text copyright © 2004 by
Steven Suskin*!*

Library of Congress Cataloging-in-Publication Data available.

ISBN 0-8118-4217-7
Manufactured in Hong Kong

Designed by
Brett MacFadden*!*
Typeset in Showcard Moderne and Gotham

Distributed in Canada by Raincoast Books
9050 Shaughnessy Street
Vancouver, British Columbia V6P 6E5

10 9 8 7 6 5 4 3 2 1

Chronicle Books LLC
85 Second Street
San Francisco, California 94105

www.chroniclebooks.com

CONTENTS

Curtain Up!

IN SOME LONG-FORGOTTEN COMEDY THAT OPENED AND INSTANTANEOUSLY SHUTTERED at the Morosco some forty years ago, an actor in a bathrobe playing an actor in a bathrobe opened his apartment door, picked up the newspaper—obviously the *Sunday New York Times*—and closed the door. Walking across the stage, he rifled through the numerous sections until he found what he was looking for. Then, unceremoniously, he dumped the rest of the paper in a strategically placed trash can.

This got a big laugh of recognition from the opening night crowd—one of the few laughs of the evening. After milking said laugh, the soon-to-be-unemployed actor opened the newspaper. He turned to the third page, folding the paper so we could see precisely what he was looking at (even from the mezzanine). Then, with a keen sense of enjoyment, he perused the ads for the new shows.

Let the world at large concentrate on the news or the markets, the obits or want ads or ball scores. For theatre fans, what is more tantalizing than that first glimpse of the ad for Broadway's next new hit?

New hit or new flop, that is. Producers and marketing folk spend an immense amount of time and concentration on these layouts and commit a large portion of their budgets to plastering the results in newspapers, on billboards, posters, and elsewhere. Nowadays they might even test-market the designs, taking a nod from big business.

But the situation remains as it always was. That first glimpse of the announcement of a new show—be it in the newspaper, on a subway platform, or inserted in the pages of a theatre program—has an immediate effect. "This one sounds good," the viewer will hopefully assert. Or maybe the reaction is adverse: "Well, I don't think I need to buy tickets to *that*." But the response that producers and ad people and theatre owners clearly bank on is "Look! This one's a must see!" That's what they want us to say, pulling out our calendars (or Blackberrys) and choosing alternate dates.

Theatrical artwork clearly represents the subject matter, content, and quality of the show at hand. That's the intention, anyway, but the reality can be somewhat less exact. More specifically, artwork often represents what the producers *intend* the show to be. And as anyone who has attended one of those surefire-hits that close before you can say *Dance of the Vampires* can attest, the side streets of Broadway are paved with intentions gone astray. It is not uncommon for producers to trade in dud artwork for a new, more effective image. Provided the play runs long enough.

There are certain basic precepts in the art of theatre art. Comedy's light and drama is dark; a cartoonish sketch with brightly colored lettering signifies one thing, a moody watercolor with stark words another. Artwork for musicals, be they brusque or arty, often signals "this is a musical": dancers sketched into the background, perhaps. (Musicals are traditionally easier to sell than comedies, which in turn are more popular than serious fare.) Cutting-edge shows might offer cutting-edge art, while offerings that are racy—or downright dirty—will be sure to convey that as a selling point. One legendary producer was convinced that the key to theatrical success was the use of a certain colored ink, which has gone down in Broadway history as "David Merrick red."

All theatre artwork is created equal, in theory, starting with a blank page and a title (often subject to change). The producer, ad agency, and artist have more options when a star is attached. A major, ticket-selling star, that is. Photos or images of stars are something prospective ticket buyers can hang on to, even if they don't remember the title of the show. Not surprisingly, most (though not all) star vehicles take full advantage of the ticket-selling luminaries above the title.

But all this talk of aims and intentions is merely theoretical. As the images in this book suggest, good shows with bland artwork are likely to do better than stinkers with glorious designs. Good theatrical artwork—meaning artwork that piques the interest, and loosens the wallets, of potential patrons—can help a show along, certainly. Bad shows, though, are rarely saved by the creativity of the designer of the artwork.

Theatrical artwork comes in various formats, each with its own distinct use. The art is usually created in the dimensions of the window card. This is a poster printed on heavy cardboard stock, roughly fourteen inches wide by twenty-two inches high. It is traditionally placed in the windows of stores and theatrical ticket brokers in the theatre districts of New York and other theatre towns across the nation. As telephone sales began to overtake in-person purchases, window cards and the street visibility they provide became less important and took up a smaller portion of a show's overall advertising budget.

Once fully designed and approved, the artwork is adapted for newspaper ads large ("display") and small ("teaser"), marquees, billboards, cover art for programs and souvenir programs, and other advertising materials. Chief among these are program inserts, or heralds. These measure six by nine, roughly the size of the programs. What better way to reach potential ticket buyers for your upcoming show than by hitting them as they sit reading during intermission at another hit show? Heralds are the least perishable items of theatrical paper and the likeliest to remain in clean condition. For these and other reasons, most of the artwork used herein is reproduced from heralds.

A Must See! includes almost two hundred pieces of theatre art. Criteria for selection varies. Some of the shows represented remain cherished memories; others are long forgotten. Legendary hits are joined by legendary failures. Many feature stars of varying stripes: old-time stage stars, iconic movie stars, stars who have long faded, and others whom readers might be surprised to find trod the boards. And then, some of the artwork was included simply for art's sake. No producer (or playwright or composer) ever aspired to artwork that was better than the production (or the script or the score). That's how things sometimes turned out, alas, as will be apparent in these pages.

I have been restricted, somewhat, by the most basic of constraints. What still exists? And in what condition? And what have I been able to put my hands on? Still, the basic criterion for all the artwork in *A Must See!* was—simply put—that it be interesting. To us, today.

The artwork is accompanied by brief captions. The format of this book does not allow for comprehensive information; my aim has been to devote as much page space as possible to the art. A few explanatory notes: I have given performance data of the New York productions, even though some of the artwork comes from pre- or post-Broadway engagements. Several of the theatres involved changed names over the decades; present-day names are included in brackets.

Critical quotes come from New York newspapers, unless specifically indicated. Drama critics who remain well-known are cited by name; these include Brooks Atkinson (of the *Times*) and Walter Kerr (of the *Herald Tribune* and, later, the *Times*), both of whom saw a theatre renamed in their honor after retirement. Otherwise, in the interest of space and concision, I simply cite the newspaper name. (Critics who are thus identified only by their employer, with apologies, include John Chapman, Robert Coleman, Robert Garland, John McClain, and Richard Watts. All are more extensively quoted, with full credit, in my books *Opening Night on Broadway* and *More Opening Nights on Broadway.*) Unattributed quotes in the captions—laudatory descriptions of the plays and players, usually—are taken from publicity materials.

The creators of the artwork are cited, when known. A fair amount of the art-work is signed (although not always legibly), and through various methods I have been able to discover the identity of other illustrators. Many, regretfully, remain unknown to us. If most of this artwork was created long ago and many of the artists are forgotten, all are much appreciated; without them, this book could not exist.

The artists who are identifiable include many of the top illustrators of their time. A few worked extensively in the theatre; most are more familiar from other fields. Among those represented are Charles Addams, Peter Arno, Ludwig Bemelmans, Jack Davis, Don Freeman, Fay Gage, Robert Galster, Bob Gill, Witold Gordon, Edward Gorey, John Held Jr., Al Hirschfeld, Hilary Knight, Oscar Liebman, Tom Morrow, Nick Nappi, Lew Parrish, Norman Rockwell, William Steig, James Thurber, Tomi Ungerer, Robert Van Nutt, Alberto Vargas, Marcel Vertès, and Tony Walton.

Much of this material hasn't been seen publicly since the shows involved opened and closed, going back to the 1920s. For my part, I am glad to help recover this ephemeral art and preserve it in a more permanent form.

So browse away, pick through these pages as if this book were an overstuffed candy box. Try to look at the artwork as if the plays were new, the songs unheard, the awards not yet awarded. Which shows look good? Which do you want to get tickets for? And which, do you suppose, will prove to be *A Must See!*

Music in the Air

THE BROADWAY MUSICAL IS THE COMMERCIAL THEATRE'S BREADWINNER. For much of the twentieth century, musical comedy was looked down upon by the lords of the legitimate drama as a frivolous, inferior art. But musicals have always been where the money is. Big money, too. By mid-century, musicals overtook and outran the most successful comedies and dramas.

Many of the musicals on the following pages were justly acclaimed as works of art. Substantial hits in their day, they toured extensively and remain popular favorites in the United States and around the world. Most made the transition to the screen, gaining exposure to a mass audience impossible to reach in the live theatre. Some of these shows have been revived on Broadway more than once and will continue to be frequent visitors in the twenty-first century.

Other Broadway musicals no longer retain their luster; they entertained the bodies in the seats at the time, and that was enough. These shows are virtually impossible to revive successfully because of weaknesses in the material, the lack of suitable stars to play the roles, or simply the passage of time. Still, all of them live on. In memory, on cast albums, and in the still-popular song hits written-to-order for the characters that populated the plots, and the original artwork that graces these pages.

THE THEATRE GUILD
PRESENTS
A NEW MUSICAL COMEDY

AWAY WE GO!

(Based on the play "GREEN GROW THE LILACS" by Lynn Riggs)

MUSIC BY
RICHARD RODGERS
BOOK AND LYRICS BY
OSCAR HAMMERSTEIN 2d
DIRECTED BY
ROUBEN MAMOULIAN
Dances by AGNES deMILLE

with

BETTY GARDE • ALFRED DRAKE • JOSEPH BULOFF • JOAN ROBERTS
LEE DIXON • HOWARD DaSILVA • CELESTE HOLM
AND A CAST OF SIXTY

Settings designed by   Costumes designed by
LEMUEL AYERS   MILES WHITE

Production under the supervision of
LAWRENCE LANGNER & THERESA HELBURN

COLONIAL THEATRE
Beginning Monday, March 15th
MATINEES THURSDAY AND SATURDAY
Prices: Evenings $3.30 to $1.10; Matinees $2.85 to $1.10

Away We Go! [Oklahoma!] 1943
St. James Theatre ★ 2,212 performances
Pre-Broadway tryout (Boston)

Away We Go! looked like just another wispy musical comedy—with a "cast of sixty"—until they changed the title in Boston and ditched this generic ad. (Due to the rarity of this artwork, we chose to reproduce a color copy from a now-vanished original.)

Oklahoma! 1943
St. James Theatre ★ 2,212 performances

"The farmer and the cowman should be friends," goes the rollicking second-act opener of Rodgers & Hammerstein's landmark musical. Witold Gordon's artwork shows us the farmer, the cowman, and their ladies. And a music-hall girl from the dream ballet assured prospective ticket buyers that the show had legs.

HAROLD PRINCE and FRED COE
present

Zero Mostel

in

Fiddler on the Roof

a new musical

Book by JOSEPH STEIN
(based on Sholem Aleichem's stories by special permission of Arnold Perl)

Music by JERRY BOCK

Lyrics by SHELDON HARNICK

with

MARIA KARNILOVA   BEATRICE ARTHUR

JOANNA   AUSTIN   BERT   JULIA
MERLIN   PENDLETON   CONVY   MAGENES

MICHAEL   JOSEPH   TANYA   ROBERT
GRANGER   SULLIVAN   EVERETT   BERDEEN

Entire Production Directed & Choreographed by
JEROME ROBBINS

Settings by   Costumes by
BORIS ARONSON   PATRICIA ZIPPRODT

Orchestrations by   Lighting by   Musical Direction & Vocal Arrangements by
DON WALKER   JEAN ROSENTHAL   MILTON GREENE

Opens Tuesday Evening, September 22
AIR
CONDITIONED   IMPERIAL THEATRE
45th St. West of Broadway -:- Matinees Wednesday and Saturday

Fiddler on the Roof 1964
Imperial Theatre ★ 3,242 performances
Preliminary artwork and credits

"Fiddler on the Roof promises to be one of New York's top song-and-dance
entries for the 1964–1965 season," said the press agent. "Wise theatregoers will
make their bookings now."

"ONE OF THE GREAT WORKS OF THE AMERICAN MUSICAL THEATRE."
—Chapman, N.Y. Daily News

HAROLD PRINCE
presents

Zero Mostel
in

Fiddler on the Roof

The New Musical Hit

Book by JOSEPH STEIN
Based on Sholom Aleichem's stories*
Music by JERRY BOCK
Lyrics by SHELDON HARNICK
with

MARIA KARNILOVA   BEATRICE ARTHUR

JOANNA   AUSTIN   BERT   JULIA
MERLIN PENDLETON CONVY MIGENES

MICHAEL   JOSEPH   TANYA   JOE
GRANGER SULLIVAN EVERETT PONAZECKI

ZVEE SCOOLER   PAUL LIPSON   GLUCK SANDOR

Entire Production Directed & Choreographed by
JEROME ROBBINS

Settings by   Costumes by   Lighting by
BORIS ARONSON   PATRICIA ZIPPRODT   JEAN ROSENTHAL

Orchestrations by   Musical Direction & Vocal Arrangements by   Dance Music Arranged by
DON WALKER   MILTON GREENE   BETTY WALBERG

Production Stage Manager RUTH MITCHELL
* (by Special Permission of Arnold Perl)   Original Cast Album — RCA Victor

IMPERIAL THEATRE
45th St. West of Broadway   -:-   Matinees Wednesday and Saturday

Fiddler on the Roof 1964
Imperial Theatre ★ 3,242 performances

Tom Morrow's artwork was quickly changed to put top-billed Zero Mostel on the roof, but he was gone within a year—because of uncontrollable scenery-chewing—and the dancing girl regained her position. Co-producer Fred Coe lost his billing prior to Broadway.

Lady Be Good! 1924
Liberty Theatre ★ 330 performances
Post-Broadway tour (Boston)

"Adele Astaire is as charming and entertaining a musical comedy actress as the town has seen on display in many a moon," said the *Times*. "Fred Astaire, too, gives a good account of himself."

Funny Face 1927
Alvin Theatre [Neil Simon] ★ 244 performances

A second hit for the Astaires and the Gershwins, despite a troubled tryout (under the title *Smarty*) that saw the departure of librettist Robert Benchley. Producers Al Aarons & Vin Freedley opened their Alvin Theatre with this "gay and tuneful" musical, although they soon lost the theatre in the Depression.

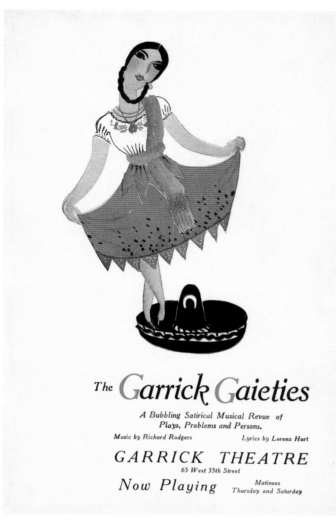

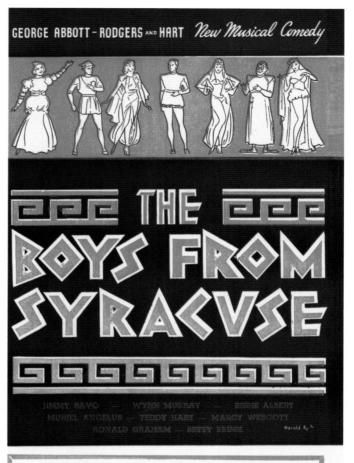

The Garrick Gaieties 1925
Garrick Theatre ★ 348 performances

This "bubbling satirical musical revue of plays, problems and persons," mounted as a two-performance benefit to raise funds for curtains for the new Guild Theatre (now the Virginia), was kept on for an extended run thanks to breezy new songwriters Rodgers & Hart. Miguel Covarrubias's artwork depicts Rosa Rolando in the second-act opener "Rancho Mexicano," for which twenty-one-year-old Mexican wunderkind Covarrubias designed sets and costumes—and he married the girl, too.

The Boys from Syracuse 1938
Alvin Theatre [Neil Simon] ★ 235 performances

"Its book is funny, its lyrics delightful, its score enchanting, its costumes and settings colorful and lovely, and its cast perfect," said the *Herald Tribune*. The design is borrowed from a Greek frieze, or perhaps a coffee shop menu.

I Married an Angel 1938
Shubert Theatre ★ 338 performances
Pre-Broadway tryout (Boston)

"A gay and capricious delight, full of jauntiness and grace and happy songs," said the *Sun*. "Pretty exactly, on the whole, what a musical comedy ought to be."

THE THEATRE GUILD, Inc. Presents

GEORGE GERSHWIN'S AMERICAN FOLK OPERA

"PORGY and BESS"

(Based on the play "Porgy")

ALVIN Theatre

52nd St., W. of B'way. Evgs. 8:30

Mat. Thursday & Saturday 2:30

Porgy and Bess 1935

Alvin Theatre [Neil Simon] ★ 124 performances

George Gershwin's "American folk opera" was a financial failure, but so were most musicals of the mid-Depression. Saddled with a large cast, a large orchestra, and a serious theme, *Porgy* lasted a mere three months but nevertheless achieved legendary status. Theatre Guild board member and resident set designer Lee Simonson provided the artwork (although he did not design the show).

"HAPPY EVENT!...

Beautiful to listen to, exciting to watch and filled with a genuineness of emotion which American lyric drama rarely offers . . . Truly it is a modern classic. . . . A splendid production of a work which the American theatre rightly loves and cherishes. . . . Beautifully acted and sung it takes on new life, excitement, passion and beauty. It is one of the few completely happy events of this dramatic season."   *Richard Watts, Jr., N. Y. Herald-Tribune*

"It triumphs in its excellent balance of story and music, in its lighter passages, in its low-down folk passages, and above all in its songs . . . One good thing keeps topping another. . . . Go see 'Porgy and Bess' if you go see nothing else."   *Louis Kronenberger, PM*

"One of the finest things in the American theatre . . . You will wait a long while before seeing again a stage full of people so gifted . . . Worth seeing over and over.
Arthur Pollock, Brooklyn Eagle

CHERYL CRAWFORD
presents

George Gershwin's

PORGY AND BESS

"Triumphantly revived!
★★★½★"
Burns Mantle, Daily News

with
TODD DUNCAN • ANNE BROWN
THE EVA JESSYE CHOIR
ALEXANDER SMALLENS, *Conductor*

"Perfect is a high-powered superlative but well merited in this case. Todd Duncan's 'Porgy' is deeply moving and beautifully sung . . . call it magnificent! Anne Brown's 'Bess' is wonderful. She has one of the best voices heard here in many semesters and her acting stirs the pulse-beat. Avon Long as 'Sportin' Life' is the most talented young Negro performer to hit Broadway in years. His 'happy dust' peddler is a gem."
Robert Coleman, Daily Mirror

"A moving, bright-hued story, told with the throbbing undercurrent of exciting music. Lusty, colorful, often barbaric. I think it's pretty grand."   *Richard Lockridge, Sun*

"A playgoer can enjoy with rhapsodic pleasure the great songs Gershwin wrote for this lovable, free-hand sketch. It is a privilege to hear them again."
Brooks Atkinson, N. Y. Times

"Alexander Smallens must be ranked as one of the noblest opera conductors of our time. He has everything: warmth and precision, heart and head."
Robert Lawrence, Music Dept.
N. Y. Herald-Tribune

"Handsomely produced and superbly sung."
John Anderson, N. Y. Journal-American

"Robert Ross' direction is full of animation, movement and engaging detail. Without question
'PORGY AND BESS' BELONGS ON YOUR 'MUST' LIST."
John Mason Brown, N. Y. World-Telegram

MAJESTIC THEATRE
West 44th Street. CI. 6-0730
Evenings 8:30—$2.75 to 55c
Matinees Wednesday and Saturday at 2:30—$2.20 to 55c
PERFORMANCE EVERY SUNDAY NIGHT — NO PERFORMANCE MONDAYS

Porgy and Bess 1942 revival
Majestic Theatre ★ 286 performances

"Better than ever," said the *Herald-Tribune* of this revival that changed the fortunes of Gershwin's opera. "Splendidly staged and beautifully acted and sung, it takes on new life, excitement, passion and beauty." Al Hirschfeld helped capture the excitement with this drawing of the hurricane scene.

"RANKS WITH THE BEST WORK ON THE AMERICAN MUSICAL STAGE."
—Brooks Atkinson, N. Y. Times

ALBERT LEWIS, in association with
VINTON FREEDLEY, presents

ETHEL WATERS

in The New Musical Triumph

"CABIN in the Sky"

Book by
LYNN ROOT • Lyrics by **JOHN LATOUCHE** • Music by **VERNON DUKE**

with **TODD DUNCAN** **DOOLEY WILSON** **REX INGRAM**
KATHERINE DUNHAM **AND HER DANCERS**

Entire Production Staged by **GEORGE BALANCHINE**

"A HIT at the MARTIN BECK . . .
what the boys call a natural . . .
★★★" *—Burns Mantle, Daily News*

"Exciting up to the final curtain. The dancing is brilliant. . . .
Miss Waters is one of the great women of the American stage."
— Richard Watts, Herald Tribune

"Joyful . . . imaginative and gay. Miss Waters has never been more engaging. Miss Dunham's dancers are something to watch."
— Richard Lockridge, N. Y. Sun

" 'Cabin in the Sky' hits a high mark. . . . Ethel Waters shines. About the most genuine Negro dancing this side of the hot countries. A swell show." *— Arthur Pollock, Brooklyn Eagle*

"Played exuberantly. Fast moving. Provides one of the most cheerful evenings on Broadway."
— Sidney Whipple, World-Telegram

"There's magic at the Beck. First nighters cheered Miss Waters and her vehicle. They shook the walls with their applause."
— Robert Coleman, Mirror

"Opened with cheers."*—Kelcey Allen, Women's Wear*

"Ethel Waters has never given a performance as rich as this before. This theatregoer imagines that he has never heard a song better sung than 'Taking A Chance On Love'. She stood that song on its head and ought to receive a Congressional Medal by way of award."
— Brooks Atkinson, N. Y. Times

MARTIN BECK THEATRE **NOW**

45th STREET WEST OF 8th AVENUE   Telephone Circle 6-6363
MATINEES WEDNESDAY AND SATURDAY

Cabin in the Sky 1940

Martin Beck Theatre [Al Hirschfeld] ★ 156 performances

"Perhaps *Cabin in the Sky* could be better than it is," suggested Brooks Atkinson, "but this correspondent cannot imagine how. It is original and joyous in an imaginative vein that suits the theatre's special genius." The artwork featured a string of Balanchine dancing girls under the gaze of Ethel Waters.

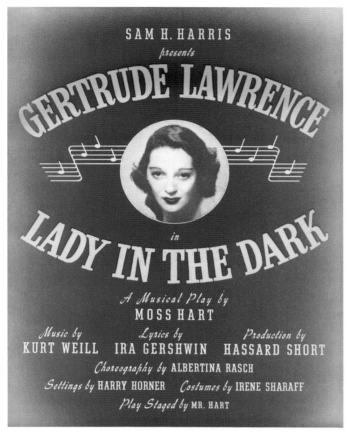

Lady in the Dark 1941
Alvin Theatre [Neil Simon] ★ 467 performances
Pre-Broadway tryout (Boston)

"Whether singing, dancing, playing emotional scenes, doing comedy or indulging in a bit of strip tease," said the *Herald Tribune,* "Gertrude Lawrence is the wonder girl of the drama season." This is a typical generic ad for a star vehicle of the time, offering Gertie's name and photo with some not-very-convincing musical notes (to alert ticket buyers that this was not simply some psychological soap opera).

Lady in the Dark 1943 return engagement
Broadway Theatre ★ 83 performances

This alternative ad displays the star in one of her jaw-dropping Hattie Carnegie gowns, during the show's "Glamour Dream" sequence.

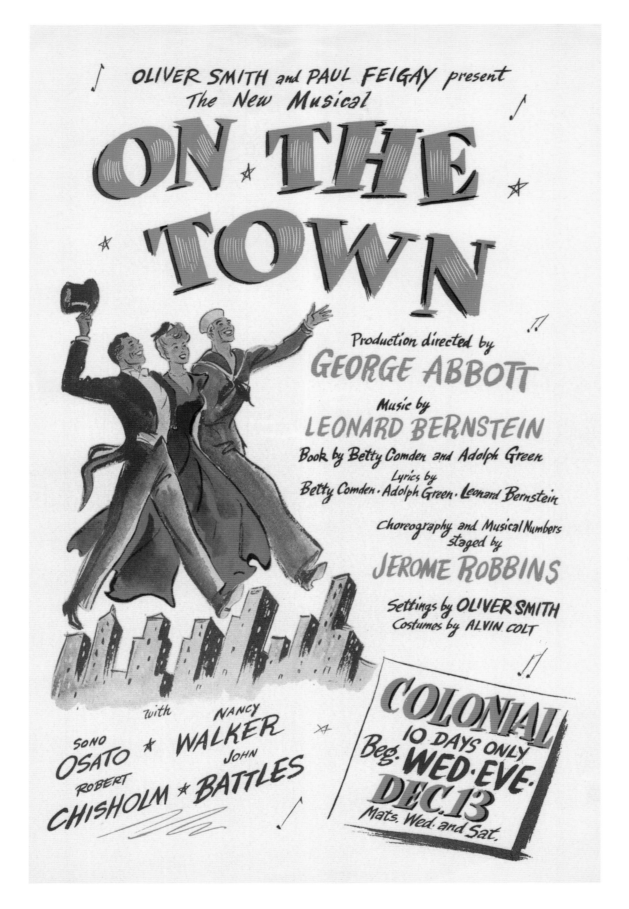

On the Town 1944
Adelphi Theatre [George Abbott] ★ 463 performances
Pre-Broadway tryout (Boston)

By the time this sleeper hit reached Broadway, the non-show-specific artwork—
top-hatted man, gowned gal, and glad-handed gob—had been replaced by
something more balletic. At the same time, the billing of composer Bernstein
and choreographer Robbins was downgraded, with Bernstein's credit as
co-lyricist removed.

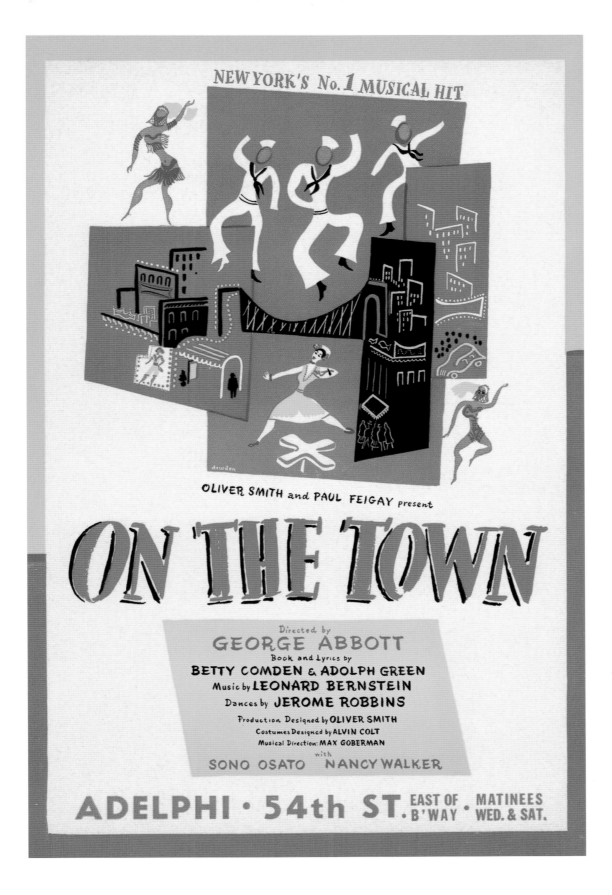

On the Town 1944
Adelphi Theatre [George Abbott] ★ 463 performances

"The freshest and most engaging musical show to come this way since
Oklahoma!" said the *Times.* "Everything about it is right, it takes neither itself
nor the world too seriously, it has wit, its dances are well paced, its players
are a pleasure to see."

MONTE and JOSEPH
PROSER KIPNESS

present

EDDIE FOY, JR.

with

JACK WHITING · AUDREY MEADOWS

IN

HIGH BUTTON SHOES

and

Ellen **HANLEY** · Frankie **HYERS** · Harry **FLEER**

MUSIC and LYRICS BY
JULE STYNE & SAMMY CAHN
BOOK BY STEPHEN LONGSTREET
PRODUCTION DESIGNED BY OLIVER SMITH
COSTUMES BY MILES WHITE
DANCES and STAGING BY DIRECTED BY
JEROME ROBBINS · GEORGE ABBOTT

*"A SONG AND DANDY
Gayer Than a Mardi Gras"
— WALTER WINCHELL*

L. A. Civic Light Opera
PHILHARMONIC AUD.

Opens Mon. Eve.
AUG. 15, 1949

NIGHTLY EXCEPT SUNDAY — MATINEES WEDNESDAY and SATURDAY
TICKETS NOW! Philharmonic Box Office, 5th and Olive Streets;
So. Calif. Music Co. Ticket Office, 737 S. Hill Street, and All Mutual Agencies

High Button Shoes 1947
Century Theatre ★ 727 performances
National tour (Los Angeles)

Don Freeman—who created the art for Pulitzer winners *The Skin of Our Teeth, A Streetcar Named Desire,* and other high-toned plays—took Jerome Robbins's madcap "Bathing Beauty Ballet" as his point of departure for this design. Comedian Phil Silvers, who originated the role of con man Harrison Floy in New York, is clearly identifiable as the snake-oil salesman on the lower right border.

On Your Toes 1936
Imperial Theatre ★ 315 performances
Post-Broadway tour (Cleveland)

"An eye-feast for the patron of the song-and-dance, girl-and-glitter type of entertainment, rich in color, costumes and lovely ladies," said the *World-Telegram*. This early piece of theatre artwork by illustrator Don Freeman named the stars but not authors Richard Rodgers, Lorenz Hart, or George Abbott.

WORLD'S FUNNIEST SHOW

GENTLEMEN PREFER BLONDES

The Laughing Saga of the Rustic Cinderella from Up Yonder . . . When she put on shoes and went to Little Rock a damned yankee DONE HER WRONG . . . But not for long . . . How she DID 'EM RIGHT makes this indeed

A MUST SEE!

GLOBE'S TRANSCENDENT
CONGRESS OF CURVACEOUS CORYPHEES

"DIAMONDS ARE A GIRL'S BEST FRIEND," carols Carol. . . . Whether it is the Kohinoor or the Cullinan or just an itsy-bittsy sparkler on the band that signifies intent to love-and-cherish, the lass with the "taking ways" is strong for the carboniferous crystal as collateral. . . . Almost as great as the yen for prized gems is the demand for Tickets to see

CAROL CHANNING

who burst on Manhattan as the predatory Lorelei from Arkin-saw with a comedy impact that brought stardom over night and the fitting accolade

FUNNIEST WOMAN ON EARTH

Gentlemen Prefer Blondes 1949
Ziegfeld Theatre ★ 740 performances
Post-Broadway tour (Chicago)

The "funniest woman on earth" plus a "transcendent congress of curvaceous coryphees," in the words of legendary press agent Dick Maney. The producers highlighted their remarkable discovery, eccentric comedienne Carol Channing, without using her likeness. Note the grapes draping the coryphées, courtesy of costume designer Miles White.

Gentlemen Prefer Blondes 1949
Ziegfeld Theatre ★ 740 performances
Post-Broadway tour (Dallas)

"Carol Channing is certainly the funniest female to hit the boards since Fannie Brice and Beatrice Lillie began knocking entire audiences out of their seats," said the *Daily News*. "The evening you go will be the holiday of the year." The producers instructed Al Hirschfeld to present a fanciful pair of gold diggers, as opposed to a caricature of their star.

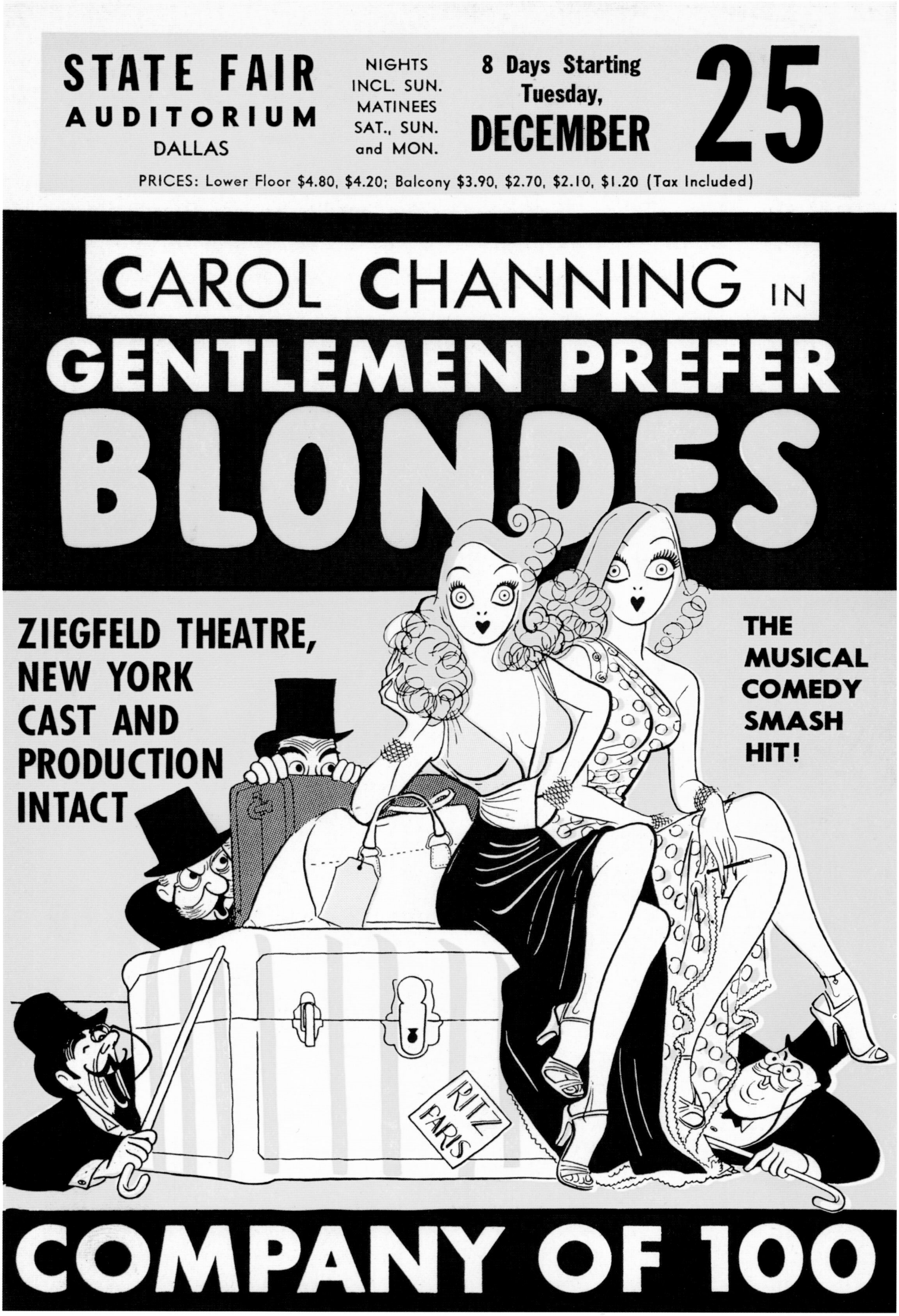
STATE FAIR
AUDITORIUM
DALLAS
NIGHTS
INCL. SUN.
MATINEES
SAT., SUN.
and MON.
8 Days Starting
Tuesday,
DECEMBER
25
PRICES: Lower Floor $4.80, $4.20; Balcony $3.90, $2.70, $2.10, $1.20 (Tax Included)
CAROL CHANNING IN
GENTLEMEN PREFER
BLONDES
ZIEGFELD THEATRE,
NEW YORK
CAST AND
PRODUCTION
INTACT
THE
MUSICAL
COMEDY
SMASH
HIT!
RITZ
PARIS
COMPANY OF 100

Kiss Me, Kate 1948
Century Theatre ★ 1,077 performances

"A rousing triumph, a gorgeous satirical musical," said the
Mirror, "it kept the first-nighters cheering wildly throughout
the proceedings. Take our advice and rush to the box office
immediately." Al Hirschfeld's bullwhip-with-heart illustration
referenced the source material, Shakespeare's *The Taming of
the Shrew.*

Guys & Dolls 1950
46th Street Theatre [Richard Rodgers] ★ 1,200 performances
National tour (Los Angeles)

"New York's own musical comedy," said the *Daily News.* "As
bright as a dime in a subway grating, as smart as a sidewalk
pigeon, as professional as Joe DiMaggio, as enchanting as the
skyline, as new as the paper you're holding."

Where's Charley? 1951 return engagement
Broadway Theatre ★ 48 performances

"Ray Bolger is not the greatest man in the world, but why quibble?"
asked the *Times.* "Bolger does virtually everything a dancer
can do except pull a ligament"—an image seemingly borrowed
from Al Hirschfeld, the resident cartoonist of the *Times.*

Annie Get Your Gun 1946
Imperial Theatre ★ 1,147 performances
Post-Broadway tour (Los Angeles)

Producers Rodgers & Hammerstein used Toni Abruzzo's non-star-specific artwork
for their big Irving Berlin musical, allowing it to be used for Mary Martin as easily
as for Ethel Merman. While Mary took *Annie* on the road, R&H wrote a new show
for her—*South Pacific.*

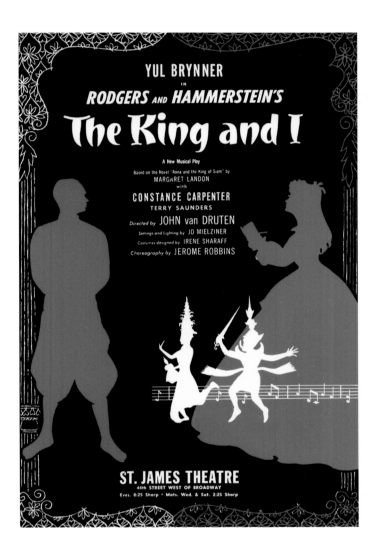

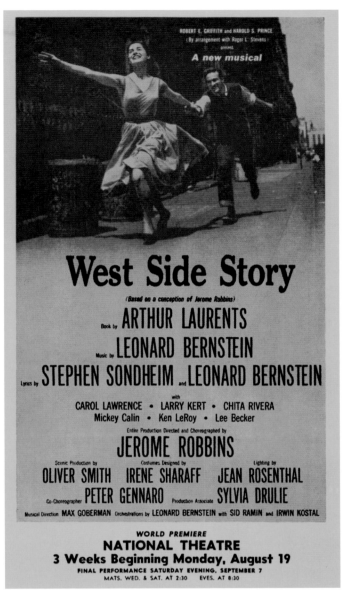

The King and I 1951
St. James Theatre ★ 1,246 performances
Replacement cast

Gertrude Lawrence, who starred as Anna and originally brought the property to Rodgers & Hammerstein, requested on her deathbed that featured player Yul Brynner (who played the King) be raised above the title. Notice how the art includes two dancing girls and a musical staff, as if to reassure audiences that this R&H musical was strong on dance and music.

West Side Story 1957
Winter Garden Theatre ★ 734 performances
Pre-Broadway tryout (Washington), preliminary credits

"Since Jerome Robbins is unquestionably the most brilliant choreographer of American musical comedy, it is a certainty that the dances will be imaginative, inventive and stirring," said the press agent. As with *On the Town,* Bernstein's initial credit as lyricist was deleted along the way.

Man and Superman 1947
Alvin Theatre [Neil Simon] ★ 295 performances
Post-Broadway tour (Chicago)

"A brilliant comedy, a brilliant performance, and a brilliant production of a great play," said the *Journal-American*. Al Hirschfeld recycled his Shaw-pulling-the strings concept a decade later for one of his most famous drawings.

My Fair Lady 1956
Mark Hellinger Theatre ★ 2,717 performances
Pre-Broadway tryout (New Haven)

"A felicitous blend of intellect, wit, rhythm and high spirits," said the *Mirror*. "A masterpiece of musical comedy legerdemain, a new landmark in the genre fathered by Rodgers and Hammerstein, a terrific show!" This photo composite was assembled by the ad agency before Rex met Julie.

NATIONAL THEATRE WASHINGTON
Limited Engagement Beg. Monday, June 20
Opening Night at 8:00; All Other Eves. at 8:30; Mats. Wed. at 2:00; Sat. at 2:30
FINAL PERFORMANCE SATURDAY NIGHT, SEPTEMBER 3rd
Mon. thru Sat. Eves.—Orch. $7.90, $6.95; 1st Balc. $6.95, $5.75, $4.30; Upper Balc. $3.00; Boxes $7.90
Wed. and Sat. Mats.—Orch. $4.95, $4.40; 1st Balc. $4.40, $3.85, $3.00; Upper Balc. $2.50; Boxes $4.95
(Tax Incl.) Make checks and money orders payable to National Theatre, 1321 E St., N.W., Wash. 4

My Fair Lady 1956
Mark Hellinger Theatre ★ 2,717 performances
National tour (Washington)

Al Hirschfeld perfectly captured the spirit of Lerner & Loewe's masterwork—
"America's greatest musical," per the press agent—which surpassed *Oklahoma!*
as Broadway's longest-running musical ever. For eight years, anyway, after it
was outrun (in quick succession) by *Hello, Dolly!* and *Fiddler on the Roof.*

DAVID MERRICK

presents

CAROL CHANNING in

The New Musical Comedy

HELLO, DOLLY!

Book by
MICHAEL STEWART

Music and Lyrics by
JERRY HERMAN

Based on "The Matchmaker" by Thornton Wilder

Also Starring

DAVID BURNS

with

EILEEN BRENNAN

SONDRA LEE

JAMES DYBAS   GORDON CONNELL   GLORIA LEROY
IGORS GAVON   ALICE PLAYTEN
and

CHARLES NELSON REILLY

Settings Designed by	Lighting by	Costumes by
OLIVER SMITH	JEAN ROSENTHAL	FREDDY WITTOP

Musical Direction and Vocal Arrangements by	Orchestrations by	Dance and Incidental Music Arranged by
SHEPARD COLEMAN	PHILIP J. LANG	PETER HOWARD

Directed and Choreographed by

GOWER CHAMPION

A David Merrick and Champion-Five Inc. Production

NATIONAL THEATRE
WASHINGTON
4 Weeks Beg. Tues. Dec. 17

MATS. WED., DEC. 18, THURS., DEC. 26, WED., JAN. 1,
WED. JAN. 8 AT 2:00 AND SATS. AT 2:30

Hello, Dolly! 1964
St. James Theatre ★ 2,844 performances
Pre-Broadway tryout (Washington), preliminary credits

"This colorful, hilarious and purely wonderful show will have you saying *Hello, Dolly!*, too," promised the press agent. The generic artwork by Knetson looks far more suited to someone like Mary Martin than *Dolly*-star Carol Channing.

Hello, Dolly! 1964
St. James Theatre ★ 2,844 performances
Pre-Broadway tryout (Washington)

"Don't bother holding onto your hats, because you won't be needing them," said Walter Kerr in the *Herald Tribune*, "you'd only be throwing them in the air anyway." Producer David Merrick chose surprisingly mild artwork for what was to be his greatest hit.

DAVID
MERRICK
presents

CAROL CHANNING in

THE NEW MUSICAL COMEDY
HELLO, DOLLY!

Book by   Music and Lyrics by

MICHAEL STEWART · JERRY HERMAN

BASED ON "THE MATCHMAKER" BY THORNTON WILDER

Also starring

DAVID BURNS

with

EILEEN BRENNAN

SONDRA LEE

and

CHARLES NELSON REILLY

Settings Designed by   Costumes by
OLIVER SMITH   FREDDY WITTOP

Lighting by   Musical Direction and Vocal Arrangements by
JEAN ROSENTHAL   SHEPARD COLEMAN

Orchestrations by   Dance & Incidental Music Arranged by
PHILIP J. LANG   PETER HOWARD

DIRECTED & CHOREOGRAPHY BY

GOWER CHAMPION

A DAVID MERRICK & CHAMPION-FIVE INC. PRODUCTION

NATIONAL THEATRE • DEC. 18 thru JAN. 11

Mats. Thurs. Dec. 19, Thurs. Dec. 26, Wed. Jan. 1, Wed. Jan. 8 at 2:00 and Sats. at 2:30

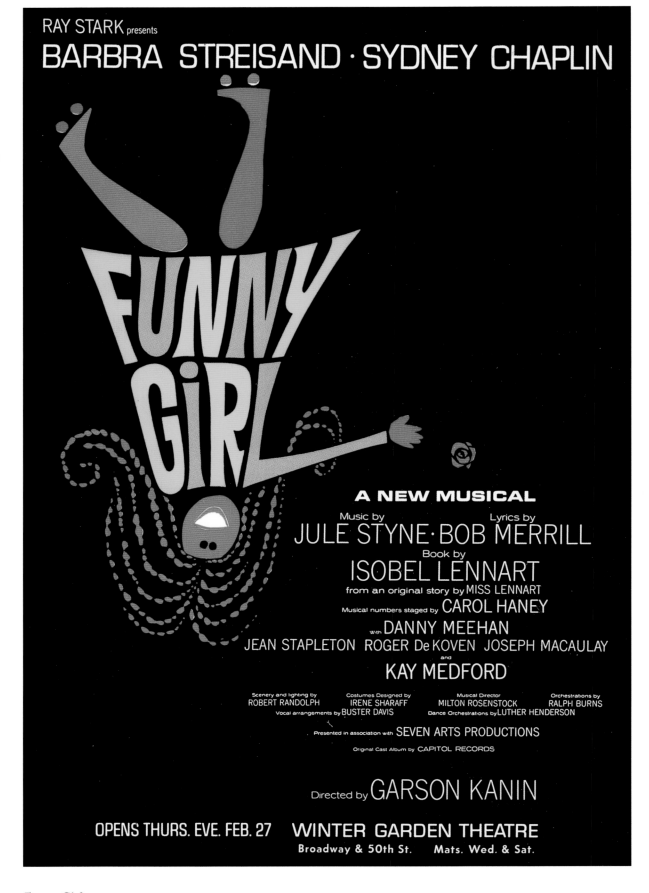

Funny Girl 1964
Winter Garden Theatre ★ 1,348 performances
Preliminary credits

"The most exciting new personality in show business, Barbra Streisand, is regarded
as the most stimulating new personality to reach Broadway in twenty years,"
said the press agent. By the time the show reached Broadway, director Jyrome
Robbins had taken over. The artwork reflects the song "I Did It on Roller Skates,"
which was cut from the show.

FRYER, CARR *and* HARRIS
present

GWEN VERDON

as

Sweet Charity

A New Musical Comedy

with
JOHN McMARTIN
and
HELEN GALLAGHER

Music by
CY COLEMAN

Lyrics by
DOROTHY FIELDS

Book by
BERT LEWIS

Based upon an original screenplay by
FEDERICO FELLINI

Scenery and Lighting by
ROBERT RANDOLPH

Costumes Designed by
IRENE SHARAFF

Musical Direction & Dance Music Arranged by
FRED WERNER

Orchestrations by
RALPH BURNS

Production Manager
ROBERT LINDEN

Associate Producer
JOHN BOWAB

Staged and Choreographed by
BOB FOSSE

Original Cast Album by COLUMBIA RECORDS

SHUBERT THEATRE
PHILADELPHIA
Mon. Dec. 6 thru Sat. Dec. 18
Opening Night at 7:30   Other Eves. at 8:30   Thurs. and Sat. Mats. at 2:00
A Theatre Guild-American Theatre Society Subscription Play

Sweet Charity 1966
Palace Theatre ★ 608 performances
Pre-Broadway tryout (Philadelphia), preliminary credits

"There are at least six things that will interest you in *Sweet Charity,*" said Walter Kerr, "the dances, the scenery, the songs, Gwen Verdon, Gwen Verdon, and Gwen Verdon." Book writer Bert Lewis (a.k.a. Robert Louis Fosse) was replaced, at his own request, by Neil Simon.

A MUST SEE!

LOW-PRICE PREVIEW OFFER

OCT. 30 thru NOV. 21

ALBERT W. SELDEN and HAL JAMES
present

RICHARD KILEY

Irving JACOBSON   Ray MIDDLETON   Robert ROUNSEVILLE

JOAN DIENER

in

ALBERT MARRE's Production

Man of La Mancha

A NEW MUSICAL PLAY

also starring
ROBERTO IGLESIAS

By DALE WASSERMAN

Music by MITCH LEIGH   Lyrics by JOE DARION

Choreography by JACK COLE

Settings and Lighting by   Costumes by
HOWARD BAY   HOWARD BAY and PATTON CAMPBELL

Musical Direction by   Musical Arrangements by
NEIL WARNER   MUSIC MAKERS, INC.

Staged by MR. MARRE

ANTA WASHINGTON SQUARE THEATRE
40 West 4th Street
Previews Oct. 30 thru Nov. 21
Eves. Tues. thru Sun.; Mats. Sat. and Sun. (no perf. Mon.)

Man of La Mancha 1965
ANTA Washington Square Theatre ★ 2,328 performances
Preliminary credits

"An exquisite musical play, the finest and most original work in our music theatre since *Fiddler on the Roof*," said the Daily News. "It moves enthrallingly from an imaginative beginning to a heart wrenching end." Roberto Iglesias—presumably the featured dancer, with sixth star billing—never made it out of rehearsal. Oscar Leibman designed the fanciful depiction of Don Quixote and Aldonza.

Man of La Mancha 1965
ANTA Washington Square Theatre ★ 2,328 performances
National tour (Washington)

After seeing the flavorful *Times* caricature, the producers replaced Oscar
Leibman's original artwork (opposite) with this Hirschfeld of stars Richard Kiley,
Joan Diener, and Irving Jacobson—and used it in New York and on the road,
regardless of star replacements.

Sam H. Harris
presents
FRANCINE LARRIMORE
in
"CHICAGO"
A New Play
by
MAURINE WATKINS
Staged by George Abbott

BOB FOSSE'S CHICAGO
A MUSICAL VAUDEVILLE

NATIONAL TOUR

CHICAGO

" 'CHICAGO' DEMANDS TO BE SEEN!"
John Simon, New York Magazine

Chicago 1926
Music Box Theatre ★ 172 performances
Post-Broadway tour (Boston)

This satirical comedy by a former reporter from the Windy City had a celebrated afterlife as a movie, a musical, and an Oscar-winning movie musical—despite an initial pan from Brooks Atkinson of the *Times* (who called it tawdry and ludicrous).

Chicago 1975
46th Street Theatre [Richard Rodgers] ★ 923 performances
National tour (Washington)

Scantily clad chorus girls show us "All That Jazz" in this big-name musical vaudeville from director-choreographer Bob Fosse, Gwen Verdon (who came up with the idea), and songwriters John Kander & Fred Ebb. The show's set designer, Tony Walton, contributed this ghostly sketch.

A Funny Thing Happened on the Way to the Forum 1962
Alvin Theatre [Neil Simon] ★ 964 performances
Pre-Broadway tryout (Washington)

"A riotous and rowdy hit," said the *Mirror,* "you won't find anything more hilarious the length of Broadway." Nick Nappi's artwork showed Zero Mostel and friend—presumably on the way *from* the forum.

A Funny Thing Happened on the Way to the Forum 1962
Alvin Theatre [Neil Simon] ★ 964 performances

This post-opening ad was designed to ensnare the tired businessman with something on his mind other than Zero Mostel. Designer Tony Walton provided the dressing.

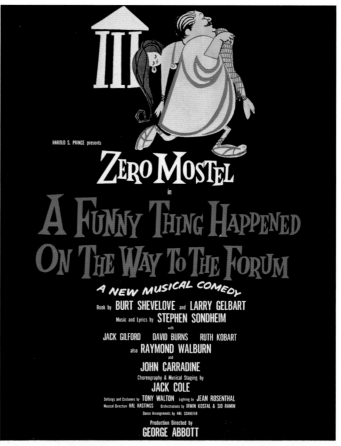

"One of the mightiest musical clicks in history"
—Walter Winchell

LEE SABINSON and WILLIAM R. KATZELL
present

FINIAN'S RAINBOW

A Completely Captivating Musical
Book by
E. Y. HARBURG and FRED SAIDY

Lyrics by   Music by
E. Y. HARBURG   BURTON LANE

Directed by
BRETAIGNE WINDUST

Scenery and Lighting by   Dances and Musical Numbers by
JO MIELZINER   MICHAEL KIDD

Costumes by   Orchestrations by
ELEANOR GOLDSMITH   ROBERT RUSSELL BENNET and DON WALKER
Vocal arrangements by LYN MURRAY

"Inspired smash musical"—NEWSWEEK

Presented by the
Los Angeles
CIVIC
LIGHT
OPERA
Association

PHILHARMONIC 4 Weeks Only Beg.
AUDITORIUM SEPT. 26

EVENINGS (Except Sunday)..............$4.80, $3.90, $3.60, $2.70, $2.40, $1.80, $1.20
POPULAR WEDNESDAY MATINEE............$3.30, $2.70, $2.40, $1.80, $1.50, $1.20
SATURDAY MATINEE $3.60, $3.00, $2.70, $1.80, $1.50, $1.20
TICKETS NOW! PHILHARMONIC BOX OFFICE, 427 West 5th Street, Los Angeles 13
Southern California Music Co., 737 South Hill, and All Mutual Agencies

Finian's Rainbow 1947
46th Street Theatre [Richard Rodgers] ★ 725 performances
National tour (Los Angeles)

Don Freeman's artwork shows Og the leprechaun watching as Susan-the-Silent dances in this "completely captivating musical." "A raree-show of enchantment, humor and beauty, to say nothing of enough social significance to hold the franchise," said Brooks Atkinson, "it puts the American musical stage several steps forward for the imagination with which it is written and for the stunning virtuosity of the performance."

Brigadoon 1947
Ziegfeld Theatre ★ 581 performances
Post-Broadway tour (Boston)

David Klein gave Lerner & Loewe's serious-themed hit bright, Scotch-plaid artwork
emphasizing the dance component of the show—and not coincidentally echoing
the dancing girl from the artwork for choreographer Agnes de Mille's *Oklahoma!*.

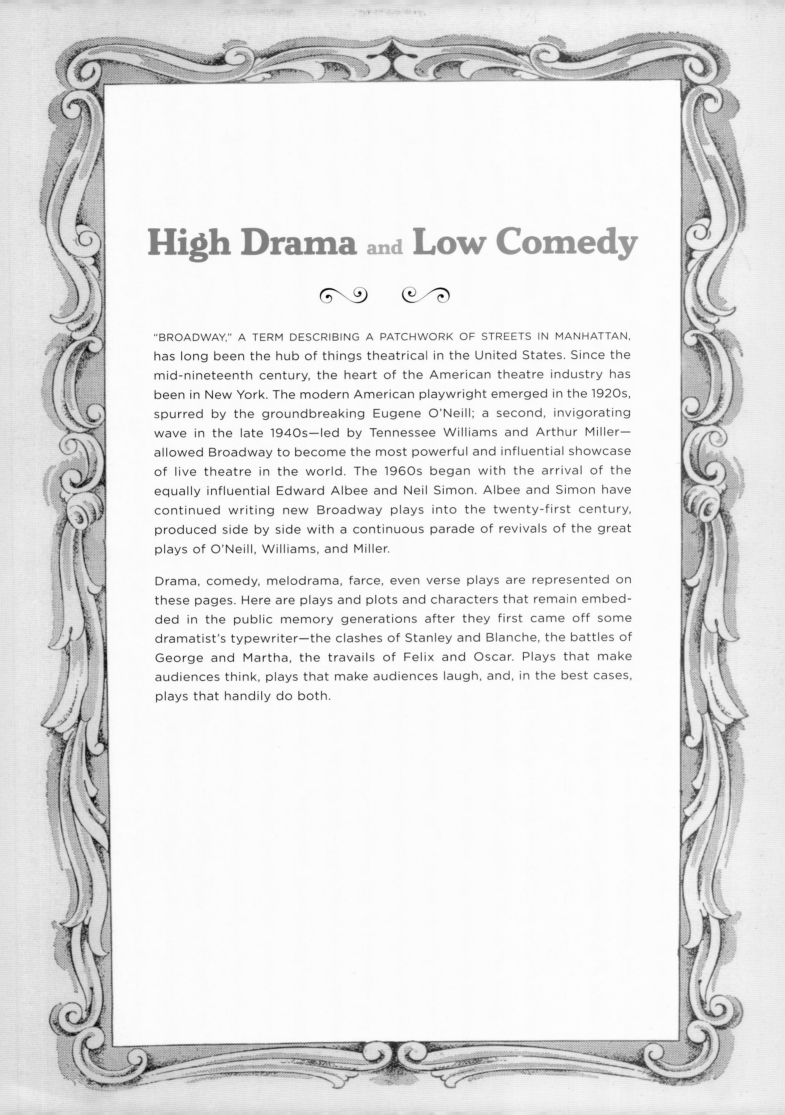

High Drama and Low Comedy

"BROADWAY," A TERM DESCRIBING A PATCHWORK OF STREETS IN MANHATTAN, has long been the hub of things theatrical in the United States. Since the mid-nineteenth century, the heart of the American theatre industry has been in New York. The modern American playwright emerged in the 1920s, spurred by the groundbreaking Eugene O'Neill; a second, invigorating wave in the late 1940s—led by Tennessee Williams and Arthur Miller—allowed Broadway to become the most powerful and influential showcase of live theatre in the world. The 1960s began with the arrival of the equally influential Edward Albee and Neil Simon. Albee and Simon have continued writing new Broadway plays into the twenty-first century, produced side by side with a continuous parade of revivals of the great plays of O'Neill, Williams, and Miller.

Drama, comedy, melodrama, farce, even verse plays are represented on these pages. Here are plays and plots and characters that remain embedded in the public memory generations after they first came off some dramatist's typewriter—the clashes of Stanley and Blanche, the battles of George and Martha, the travails of Felix and Oscar. Plays that make audiences think, plays that make audiences laugh, and, in the best cases, plays that handily do both.

KERMIT BLOOMGARDEN and WALTER FRIED
present
ELIA KAZAN'S production of

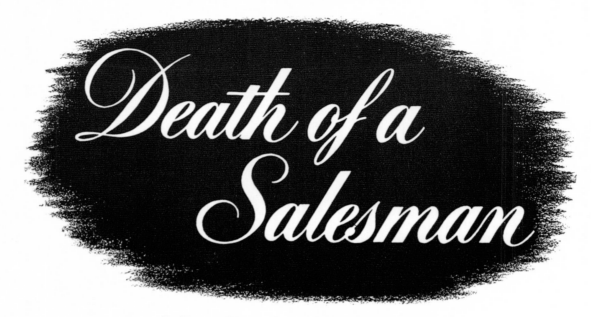

Death of a Salesman

A New Play by ARTHUR MILLER
Staged by ELIA KAZAN
with

LEE J. **COBB** · ARTHUR **KENNEDY**

MILDRED **DUNNOCK** · HOWARD **SMITH** · THOMAS **CHALMERS**

CAMERON **MITCHELL** · ALAN **HEWITT**

DON KEEFER · WINNIFRED CUSHING · TOM PEDI
CONSTANCE FORD · ANNE DRISCOLL · PEGGY MEREDITH

Setting and Lighting by JO MIELZINER

Music Composed by ALEX NORTH   *Costumes by* JULIA SZE

LOCUST ST. THEATRE
PHILADELPHIA
2 Weeks, Beg. Saturday Evening, January 22
MATINEES THURSDAY and SATURDAY

Death of a Salesman 1949
Morosco Theatre ★ 742 performances
Pre-Broadway tryout (Philadelphia)

"At thirty-three Arthur Miller has been accepted as one of the very few important
playwrights in our theatre today, and as a novelist of great promise." So opined
the press agent, before *Death of a Salesman* first took the stage.

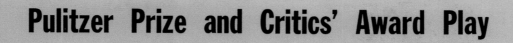

Pulitzer Prize and Critics' Award Play

KERMIT BLOOMGARDEN & WALTER FRIED

PRESENT

THOMAS MITCHELL

in

ELIA KAZAN'S
production of

death of a Salesman

by ARTHUR MILLER

Setting and Lighting by
JO MIELZINER

COX THEATRE
CINCINNATI
1 Week Beg. Monday, February 27
MATINEES WEDNESDAY and SATURDAY
4th Play Theatre Guild-American Theatre Society Subscription Series

Death of a Salesman 1949
Morosco Theatre ★ 742 performances
National tour (Cincinnati)

"A poignant, shattering and devastating drama," said the *Sun*. "When the living theatre soars it dwarfs all competitive mediums; it soared last night." Joseph Hirsch's slump-shouldered salesman in retreat, modeled after the performance of Lee J. Cobb, perfectly captured the spirit of Willy Loman.

Our Town 1938
Morosco Theatre ★ 336 performances

"A hauntingly beautiful play," said Brooks Atkinson, "*Our Town*
has escaped from the formal barrier of the modern theatre
into the quintessence of acting, thought and speculation." With
a set of reviews like this, producer Jed Harris understandably
settled on a straight quote ad.

Broadway 1926
Broadhurst Theatre ★ 603 performances
National tour (Boston)

This fast and furious melodrama of the speakeasy and cabaret
was an extraordinary success, bringing immediate fame to
producer Jed Harris and author George Abbott and serving as
the model for a whole genre of gangster films.

Angel Street 1941
John Golden Theatre ★ 1,295 performances

"The best, most uncompromising and most tingling thriller
which has been presented hereabouts," said the *World-
Telegram* about this "almost unbearably nerve-racking"
melodrama (also known as *Gaslight*). The artwork shows Judith
Evelyn cowering beneath the manipulative Vincent Price.

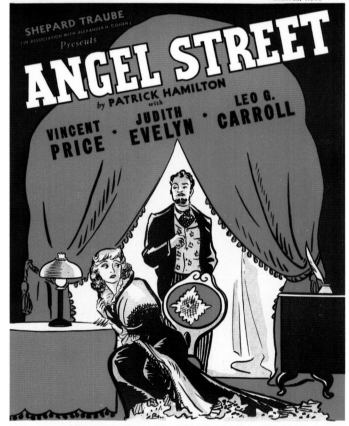

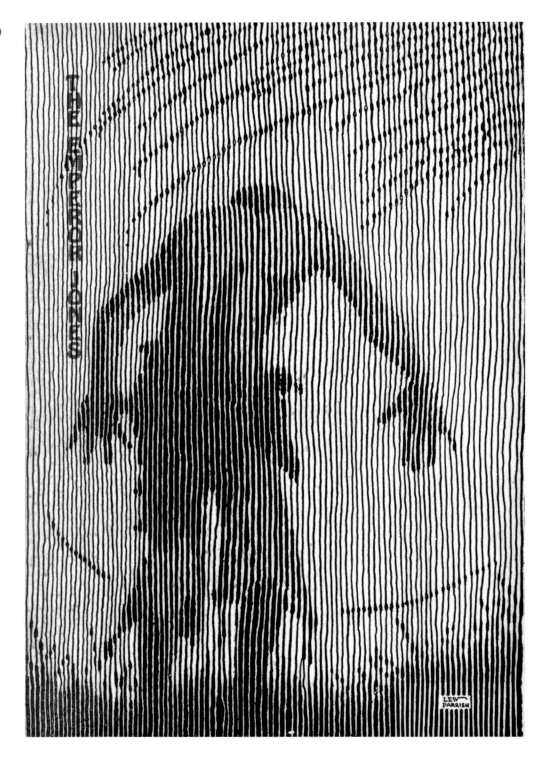

The Emperor Jones 1920
Neighborhood Playhouse ★ 204 performances
Post-Broadway tour (Cleveland)

"An extraordinarily striking and dramatic story," said Alexander Woollcott in the
Times, "for strength and originality, Eugene O'Neill has no rival among the
American writers for the stage." O'Neill cemented his reputation with his second
hit of the year, following the Pulitzer Prize–winning *Beyond the Horizon.* The play
climaxes with the Emperor Jones pursued through a forest of shadowy darkness
and brutal terror, as captured by illustrator Lew Parrish.

"The first major event of the season." —*Brooks Atkinson, N. Y. Times.*

GUTHRIE McCLINTIC
PRESENTS
MAXWELL ANDERSON'S
WINTERSET

MARTIN BECK THEATRE 45 ST. W. OF 8 AVE.
MATS. WED. & SAT.

"One of the finest plays which any American has ever written."
—*Gilbert Gabriel, N. Y. American*

Winterset 1935
Martin Beck Theatre [Al Hirschfeld] ★ 194 performances

"*Winterset* lives on a plane of high thinking, deep emotion and eloquent writing," said Brooks Atkinson, "it is a courageous poem to justice and integrity; in short, it is beautiful." Matching the stage poetry was Jo Mielziner's setting, with a glimmer of sky overwhelmed by the massive Brooklyn Bridge. At the far right are stars Burgess Meredith (first) and Richard Bennett (third), while the actress billed simply as Margo stands framed in the daylight.

Max Gordon
presents
THE WOMEN

A NEW COMEDY BY
CLARE BOOTHE
CAST OF 40 • ALL WOMEN

The Women 1936
Ethel Barrymore Theatre ★ 657 performances

"It will delight the feminine spectators by convincing them
that they are witty and it will flatter the men and it will make a
million dollars for its author and producer," said the *Herald
Tribune.* Playwright Clare Boothe [Luce] took male spectators
inside the sacred precincts of beauty salons and powder rooms,
as promised by the artwork.

The Little Foxes 1939
National Theatre [Nederlander] ★ 410 performances
Post-Broadway tour (Washington)

Tallulah Bankhead—peering imperiously as the malevolent
Regina Hubbard Giddens from a photo from Florence
Vandamm—had her greatest role in this "grim, bitter and
merciless study," which the *Herald Tribune* called "a drama
more honest, more pointed and more brilliant than even [Lillian]
Hellman's triumphant previous work, *The Children's Hour.*"

The Greatest Play of the Generation!

HERMAN SHUMLIN
PRESENTS

TALLULAH BANKHEAD

in *The*

LITTLE FOXES

LILLIAN HELLMAN'S DRAMATIC TRIUMPH

WITH

FRANK CONROY

STAGED BY MR. SHUMLIN

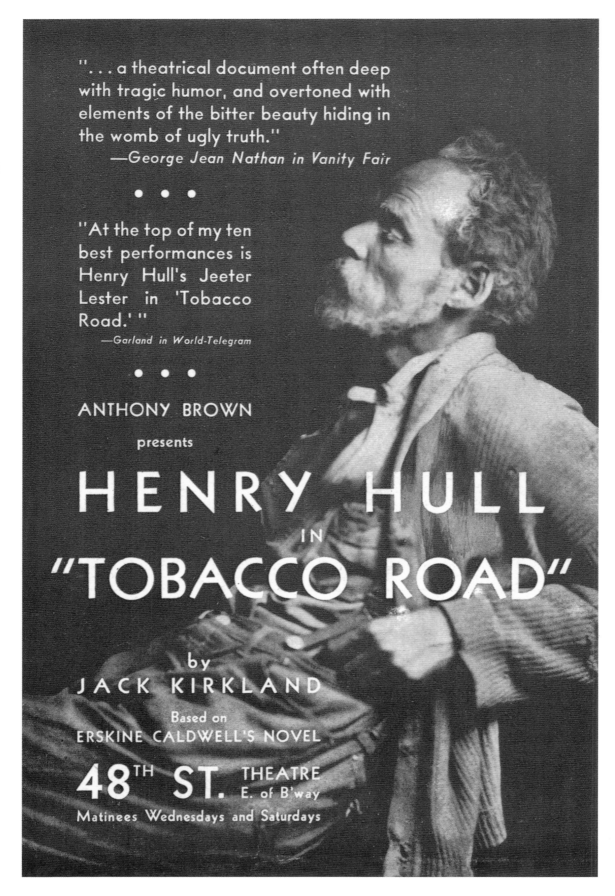

"...a theatrical document often deep with tragic humor, and overtoned with elements of the bitter beauty hiding in the womb of ugly truth."
—*George Jean Nathan in Vanity Fair*

• • •

"At the top of my ten best performances is Henry Hull's Jeeter Lester in 'Tobacco Road.' "
—*Garland in World-Telegram*

• • •

ANTHONY BROWN
presents

HENRY HULL
IN
"TOBACCO ROAD"
by
JACK KIRKLAND
Based on
ERSKINE CALDWELL'S NOVEL

48TH ST. THEATRE
E. of B'way
Matinees Wednesdays and Saturdays

Tobacco Road 1933
Masque Theatre [John Golden] ★ 3,182 performances

"An ugly wallowing sort of drama that not only strengthens your disgust with specific examples of the so-called human race, but also gives you a certain feeling of verminous contact with it," said the *Daily News*. With reviews like this, *Tobacco Road* was an immediate smash hit and remains Broadway's second-longest-running play ever.

All-American Record Breaker!

OSCAR SERLIN *presents* CLARENCE DAY'S

LIFE WITH FATHER

Made into a play by
HOWARD LINDSAY and RUSSEL CROUSE

DIRECTED BY BRETAIGNE WINDUST   SETTING AND COSTUMES BY STEWART CHANEY

"If You Want to Laugh and Laugh and Laugh By All Means See 'LIFE WITH FATHER!' Public Entertainment Number One!"
—WALTER WINCHELL

Life with Father 1939
Empire Theatre ★ 3,224 performances
National tour (Philadelphia)

"A darlin' play, overpoweringly funny," said Brooks Atkinson of this comedy that surpassed *Tobacco Road* to become Broadway's longest-running non-musical. Based on a series of stories by Clarence Day that originally appeared in the *New Yorker,* the producer commissioned artwork from popular *New Yorker* illustrator Will Cotton.

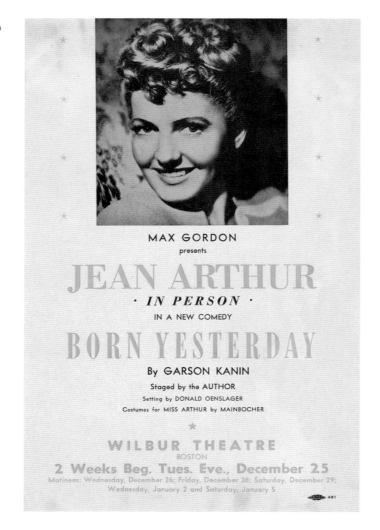

Born Yesterday 1946
Lyceum Theatre ★ 1,641 performances
Pre-Broadway tryout (Boston), preliminary credits

Hollywood favorite Jean Arthur withdrew in stage fright during the Boston tryout, leaving *Born Yesterday* in desperate shape—until the unknown Judy Holliday stepped in, propelling it into the biggest hit of the early post–World War II years (with a motion picture sale of a cool million).

Born Yesterday 1946
Lyceum Theatre ★ 1,641 performances
National tour (Boston)

"A tough, tender, terrifying showpiece with everything to recommend it to the theatregoer in search of entertainment, enlightenment, or a swift kick in the great American complacence," said the *Journal-American*.

The Rainmaker 1954
Cort Theatre ★ 125 performances
Pre-Broadway tryout (Philadelphia)

"A cloudburst of a hit," said the *World-Telegram,* "Geraldine Page really spread her wings last night. She has been billed as a star before, now she declares that stardom irrevocably."

The Rainmaker 1954
Cort Theatre ★ 125 performances
Post-Broadway tour (Washington)

Facing poor business, the producers shifted the emphasis by capitalizing on Geraldine Page—who received far more enthusiastic reviews than the play itself—with this tempestuous photo ad.

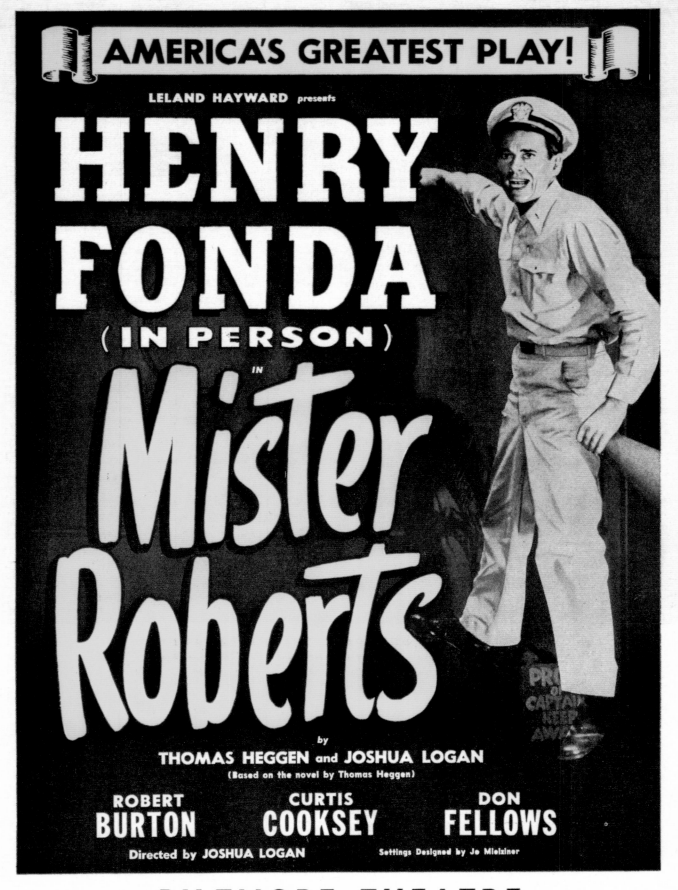

Mister Roberts 1948
Alvin Theatre [Neil Simon] ★ 1,157 performances
Post-Broadway tour (Los Angeles)

"A magnificent play with heart, humor, profound meaning and an almost intolerable emotional tension," said the *Herald Tribune,* "a tumultuous and moving drama that no one who witnesses will soon forget." Henry Fonda, at the height of his popularity, helped make the show into an event.

Two for the Seesaw 1958
Booth Theatre ★ 750 performances
Pre-Broadway tryout (Washington)

"A bombshell of emotion and hilarity, a whale of a hit," said the *Mirror,* hailing the unknown Anne Bancroft as "the most engaging gamin to light up a stage in many a semester."

The Miracle Worker 1959
Playhouse Theatre ★ 719 performances
Pre-Broadway tryout (Philadelphia)

"Powerful, hair-raising, spine-tingling, touching, and just plain wonderful," said Walter Kerr of this play about Helen Keller and her teacher, Annie Sullivan, "but it's not a miracle, it's honesty and talent." Rather than illustrating the difficult subject matter, the pre-Broadway ad featured publicity photos of the stars and omitted any mention of Keller.

SAINT SUBBER
IN ASSOCIATION WITH
ELIA KAZAN
PRESENTS

WILLIAM INGE'S

NEW PLAY

THE DARK AT THE TOP OF THE STAIRS

DIRECTED BY

ELIA KAZAN

WITH

TERESA WRIGHT PAT HINGLE EILEEN HECKART

FRANK OVERTON   CAROL LYNLEY   TIMMY EVERETT

JUDITH ROBINSON   CHARLES SAARI   CARL REINDEL

Setting by BEN EDWARDS
Costumes by LUCINDA BALLARD
Lighting by JEAN ROSENTHAL

SHUBERT THEATRE
NEW HAVEN
THURS., FRI., SAT.
NOVEMBER 7th, 8th, 9th
EVES. AT 8:30 -:- MAT. SAT. AT 2:30

The Theatre Guild and Joshua Logan
present
"PICNIC"

A New Play *by* **William Inge**
(Author of ''Come Back, Little Sheba'')

with

RALPH MEEKER • JANICE RULE
EILEEN HECKART • KIM STANLEY • ARTHUR O'CONNELL
and **PEGGY CONKLIN**

Directed by
JOSHUA LOGAN

Setting designed by **Jo Mielziner**

HARTMAN THEATRE COLUMBUS • 3 Days Beg. Thurs., January 15

MATINEE SATURDAY

PRICES (Including All Taxes): Eves. - Orch. & Boxes $3.75; Balc. $3.10, $2.50
Saturday Matinee - Orch. & Boxes $3.10; Balc. $2.50, $1.90
Evenings & Matinee - 2nd Balcony Seats Not Reserved, **Not Sold By Mail**, $1.90
A Theatre Guild-American Theatre Society Subscription Play

The Dark at the Top of the Stairs 1957
Music Box Theatre ★ 468 performances
Pre-Broadway tryout (New Haven), preliminary credits

"A stirring adventure in playgoing," said the *Mirror.* "Though it is tensely dramatic, it is packed with laughs tinged with tears; it will make you roar one minute and cry the next." Playwright William Inge presented his family drama through the eyes of children, as in the artwork by Robert Galster.

Picnic 1953
Music Box Theatre ★ 477 performances
Pre-Broadway tryout (Columbus, Ohio)

"This William Inge knows how to write," said the *Post.* "Excellently acted and sympathetically staged, Inge's new work reveals power, insight, compassion, observation and a gift for looking into the human heart." Before the reviews came out, this rehearsal photo helped sell tickets (while newcomer Paul Newman went unbilled).

A MUST SEE!

Exclusive Pre-Broadway Engagement

Cheryl Crawford

presents

PAUL NEWMAN **SIDNEY BLACKMER** **GERALDINE PAGE**

in

SWEET BIRD OF YOUTH

A New Play by
TENNESSEE WILLIAMS

Directed by
ELIA KAZAN

Settings and Lighting by **JO MIELZINER**
Costumes by **ANNA HILL JOHNSTONE**

WILLIAM GOLDMAN
NEW LOCUST •
Broad & Locust—PE 5-5074

OPENS MON. FEB. 9
3 Weeks Only

Eves. at 8:30—Mats. Thurs., Feb. 12, 19, and Mon., Feb. 23 (Washington's Birthday) and Sats. at 2:30

Sweet Bird of Youth 1959
Martin Beck Theatre [Al Hirschfeld] ★ 375 performances
Pre-Broadway tryout (Philadelphia)

"A play of overwhelming force," said the *Post,* "brilliantly staged and acted, written with the enormous dramatic drive, the sense of darkly brooding lyricism, and the gift for presenting a baleful atmosphere of malignant evil for which Williams is famous." As was typical, the early ads for the out-of-town tryout featured publicity photos of the stars.

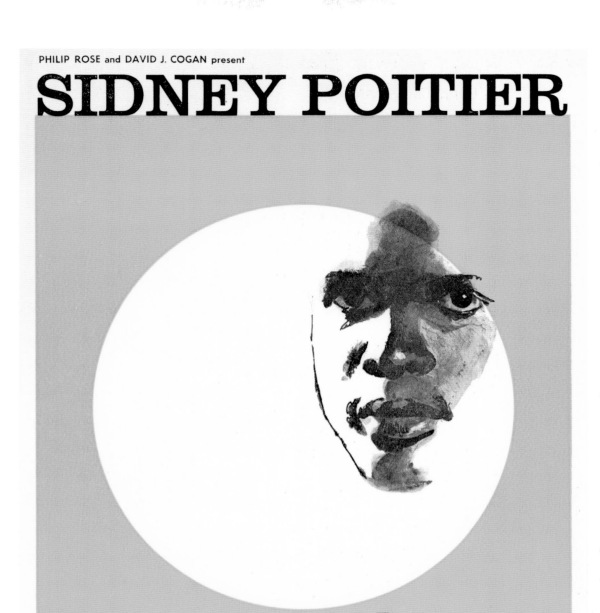

PHILIP ROSE and DAVID J. COGAN present

SIDNEY POITIER

a raisin in the sun

A new play by LORRAINE HANSBERRY

with

CLAUDIA McNEIL   RUBY DEE
LOUIS GOSSETT   DIANA SANDS

Directed by LLOYD RICHARDS
Designed and Lighted by RALPH ALSWANG
Costumes by VIRGINIA VOLLAND

WALNUT ST. THEATRE — 2 Weeks Beg. Mon. Jan. 26
PHILADELPHIA   Matinees Wednesday and Saturday

A Raisin in the Sun 1959
Ethel Barrymore Theatre ★ 530 performances
Pre-Broadway tryout (Philadelphia)

"History was made last night," said the *Journal-American.* "A play by a Negro about Negroes with an almost all-Negro cast opened on Broadway and was a stupendous, unsegregated hit." The striking portrait of star Sidney Poitier can be viewed, literally, as a raisin in the sun.

A MUST SEE!

THE HILARIOUS COMEDY HIT
DIRECT FROM A YEAR IN NEW YORK

"DELIRIOUSLY DAFFY"
—COLEMAN, N. Y. MIRROR

PHOENIX THEATRE
by arrangement with ROGER L. STEVENS
presents

JEROME ROBBINS'
PRODUCTION

HERMIONE GINGOLD

in

"OH DAD, POOR DAD, MAMMA'S HUNG YOU
IN THE CLOSET AND I'M FEELIN' SO SAD"

By ARTHUR KOPIT

with ALIX ELIAS   SAM WATERSTON
and SANDOR SZABO

Originally Directed by JEROME ROBBINS

Scenery by	Costumes by	Lighting by	Music by
William & Jean Eckart	Patricia Zipprodt	Thomas Skelton	Robert Prince

"FUNNY & NONSENSICAL"
—TAUBMAN, N. Y. TIMES

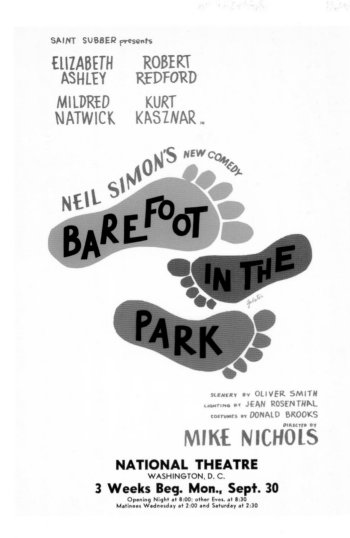

Barefoot in the Park 1963
Biltmore Theatre ★ 1,532 performances
Pre-Broadway tryout (Washington)

"The funniest comedy I can remember, it's as simple as that," said the *Journal-American* of this Neil Simon–Mike Nichols laugh hit. "It's so good it looks easy." Note Robert Galster's humorous effect of the three-footed graphic with uneven lettering.

The Odd Couple 1965
Plymouth Theatre ★ 964 performances
Pre-Broadway tryout (Washington)

This second—and heartier—comedy hit from Simon & Nichols was "wildly, irresistibly, incredibly and continuously funny," said the *Daily News,* "which doesn't leave me with much else to say, does it?" Robert Galster's artwork takes its lead from the memorable poker game in the first scene.

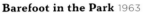

Oh Dad, Poor Dad 1962
Phoenix Theatre ★ 454 performances
National tour (Indianapolis)

Arthur Kopit's avant-garde "pseudoclassical tragifarce in a bastard French tradition," under the direction of Jerome Robbins, helped prepare New York audiences for Edward Albee's *Who's Afraid of Virginia Woolf?* later that year. Artwork for the road tour pointed up the "deliriously daffy" quote.

A MUST SEE!

"INDEED THE BEST AMERICAN PLAY FOR SOME FEW SEASONS. SCREAMINGLY FUNNY!"
—Clive Barnes, New York Times

"COMIC BRILLIANCE!"
—Newsweek

"LANCING WIT!"
—Time Magazine

THE BOYS IN THE BAND

A New Play by
MART CROWLEY

Directed by
ROBERT MOORE

Production Designed by
PETER HARVEY

NATIONAL THEATRE
1321 E. ST., N.W.   WASHINGTON, D.C. 20004

Monday, June 30 thru Saturday, July 26

All Evenings at 7:30   Matinees Wed and Sat. at 2:00
Prices: Mon.-Thurs. Evenings Orch. $6.50; 1st Balc. $6.50, 5.50, 4.50; Upper Balc. $2.50
Fri. and Sat. Evenings Orch. $7.50; 1st Balc. $7.50, 6.50, 5.50; Upper Balc. $3.00
Wed. and Sat. Matinees Orch. $5.50; 1st Balc. $5.50, 4.50, 3.00; Upper Balc. $1.95

The Boys in the Band 1968
Theatre Four ★ 1,000 performances
National tour (Washington)

"It is not—repeat not—for adults who are unsophisticated or unprepared; it will shock many playgoers as they have never before been shocked," said Elliot Norton in the *Boston Record-American*.

MAIL ORDERS NOW FOR NEW YORK'S

MOST PRAISED
MOST TALKED-ABOUT
MOST EXCITING
PLAY OF THE YEAR

"IT MUST BE SEEN!"   "NOTHING SHORT OF TREMENDOUS!"
—Kerr, N.Y. Herald Tribune   —Taubman, N.Y. Times

"TOWERS OVER THE COMMON RUN OF CONTEMPORARY PLAYS!"
—Watts, N.Y. Post

EVERY EVENING AT 8:00 SHARP!

UTA HAGEN · ARTHUR HILL · BEN PIAZZA

in EDWARD ALBEE'S

WHO'S AFRAID OF VIRGINIA WOOLF?

with   directed by
Melinda Dillon   Alan Schneider

Mats Wed. &   with   KATE REID · SHEPPERD STRUDWICK
Sat. at 2:00

BILLY ROSE THEATRE 212 W. 41st St., N.Y. 36

Who's Afraid of Virginia Woolf? 1962
Billy Rose Theatre [Nederlander] ★ 644 performances

"A horror play written by a humorist, a decline-of-the-western," said Walter Kerr,
"it is a brilliant piece of writing, with a sizable hole in its head; it need not be
liked, but it must be seen." The producers used a simple ad with stark lettering to
suggest the play's jolting impact.

The Time of Your Life 1939
Booth Theatre ★ 185 performances

"A sort of cosmic vaudeville show," said the *Herald Tribune*. "A helter-skelter mixture of humor, sentimentalism, philosophy and melodrama, and one of the most enchanting theatrical works imaginable." Illustrator Don Freeman provided the artwork for three groundbreaking Pulitzer Prize–winners within the decade.

The Skin of Our Teeth 1942
Plymouth Theatre ★ 355 performances

"Thornton Wilder's dauntless and heartening comedy stands head and shoulders above anything ever written for our stage," said Alexander Woollcott in the *Times*. Don Freeman's artwork shows Tallulah Bankhead and her costars (and household pets) escaping the Ice Age by the skin of their teeth.

A Streetcar Named Desire 1947
Ethel Barrymore Theatre ★ 855 performances
National tour (Pittsburgh)

Don Freeman's artwork has Stanley Kowalski watch as Blanche DuBois awaits *A Streetcar Named Desire.* "Feverish, squalid, tumultuous, painful, steadily arresting and oddly touching," said the *Post.* "Despite the blackness of fate that Williams depicts, there is a frequent quality of lyric originality in his pessimism that gives it an inescapable vitality."

Winner of PULITZER PRIZE
and CRITICS' AWARD for
The Best Play of the Year

IRENE M. SELZNICK
presents
ELIA KAZAN'S PRODUCTION OF

A STREETCAR NAMED DESIRE

by

TENNESSEE WILLIAMS

Directed by MR. KAZAN

with

UTA HAGEN · ANTHONY QUINN

Setting and Lighting by JO MIELZINER
Costumes Designed by LUCINDA BALLARD

NIXON THEATRE
PITTSBURGH

2 Weeks, Beginning Monday, September 6

MATINEES WEDNESDAY and SATURDAY

Star Quality

BROADWAY SHOWS LIVE AND DIE ON TICKET SALES. Nobody has ever been able to determine just what will make a person buy a theatre ticket; otherwise, there'd be someone out there who's never had a failure. But of all the variables that affect ticket sales—or the lack of same—the most significant one is the presence of a ticket-selling star.

Stars, and star vehicles, come in numerous stripes. A brilliant play or musical usually comes across as a brilliant play or musical with or without a star (although a star can help ease acceptance). A mediocre play or musical can be built to fit around a star. With luck, the presence of said luminary—live on stage, as they say in the ads—is enough to tip the scales. And then there is material that is downright poor, doomed to fail no matter who plays it. All of these star vehicles started with the same advantage: a famous and familiar face for prospective ticket buyers to latch on to. An advantage that lasted until the night of the first performance, that is, when the curtain went up and the material itself was revealed.

Major stars work on Broadway for any number of reasons. There is the stage star tried and true, such as Helen Hayes or Mary Martin, for whom no other medium would do. There is the movie star with stage origins, such as Katharine Hepburn or Henry Fonda, who returns to the stage whenever his or her schedule (and agent) allows. And there is the fading star, who visits Broadway in an attempt at career resuscitation. Sometimes—as in the cases of Lauren Bacall and Robert Preston—it even works!

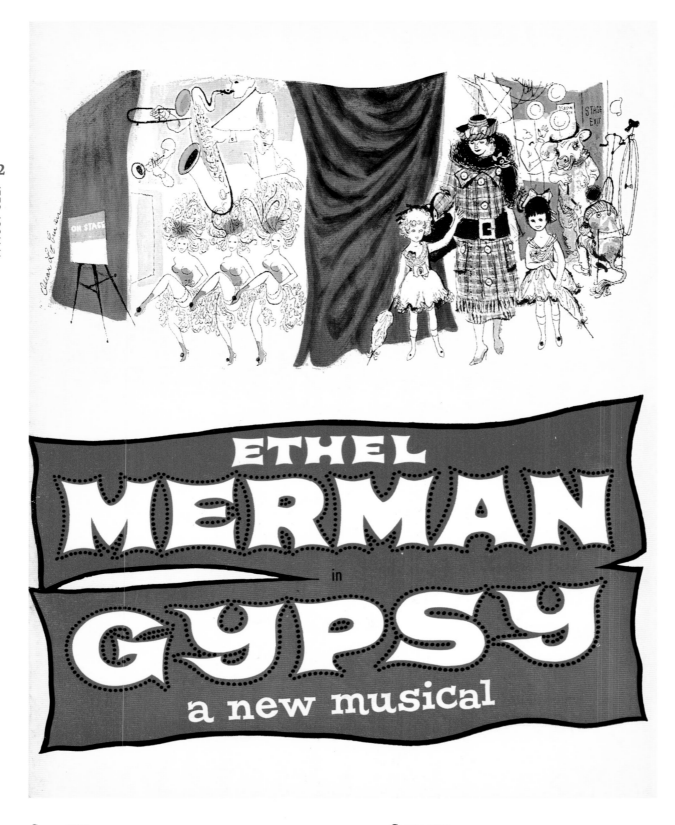

Gypsy 1959
Broadway Theatre ★ 702 performances

"I'm not sure whether *Gypsy* is new-fashioned or old-fashioned
or integrated or non-integrated," said Walter Kerr. "The only
thing I'm sure of is that it's the best damn musical I've seen
in years." Oscar Leibman's atmospheric sketch (above) of the
dual backstage worlds effectively captured the backstage
milieu. People familiar with the show will notice Caroline the
cow on the far right, smoking a cigar.

Gypsy 1959
Broadway Theatre ★ 702 performances

The artistic original art didn't help sell tickets, so the
producers switched to the hard sell with a photo of their
star, Ethel Merman.

"BEST DAMN MUSICAL I'VE SEEN IN YEARS!"

— KERR, N. Y. Herald-Tribune

DAVID MERRICK and **LELAND HAYWARD**
present

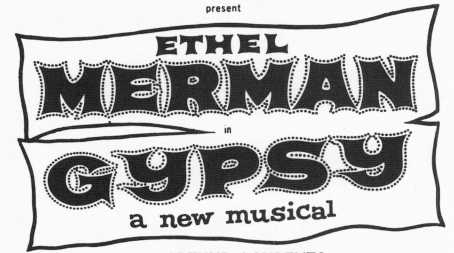

ETHEL
MERMAN
in
Gypsy
a new musical

Book by **ARTHUR LAURENTS**
Music by **JULE STYNE**
Lyrics by **STEPHEN SONDHEIM**

Suggested by the Memoirs of **GYPSY ROSE LEE**

Costumes Designed by   Settings and Lighting by
JO MIELZINER   **RAOUL PÈNE DU BOIS**

ENTIRE PRODUCTION DIRECTED AND CHOREOGRAPHED BY
JEROME ROBBINS

Musical Direction by   Orchestrations by   Dance Music Arranged by
MILTON ROSENSTOCK   **SID RAMIN** with Robert Ginzler   **JOHN KANDER**

Red, Hot and Blue! 1936
Alvin Theatre [Neil Simon] ★ 183 performances

Merman, Durante, and Hope headed Cole Porter's "De-Lovely" romp, which George Jean Nathan commended "to the paying attention of all lovers of the serious drama who can't find any decent serious drama around these days to spend their money on." Jimmy and Ethel had both been promised top billing, resulting in this Solomonic crisscross.

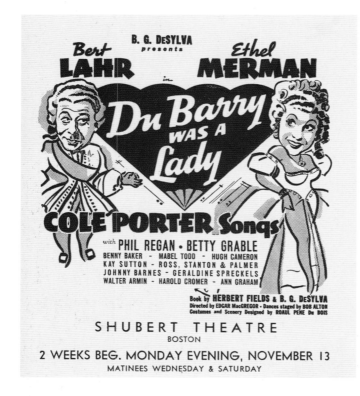

DuBarry Was a Lady 1939
46th Street Theatre [Richard Rodgers] ★ 408 performances
Pre-Broadway tryout (Boston), preliminary credits

Bert Lahr (just off *The Wizard of Oz*) played Louis XIV to Ethel Merman's DuBarry in this rowdy Cole Porter musical about a nightclub men's room attendant who is transported to Versailles by a self-inflicted Mickey Finn.

Panama Hattie 1940
46th Street Theatre [Richard Rodgers] ★ 501 performances

"A roaring musical, vastly entertaining," said Brooks Atkinson of this wartime hit (despite a lackluster Cole Porter score). This simplistic artwork only vaguely resembles star Ethel Merman, but no matter.

Idiot's Delight 1936
Shubert Theatre ★ 300 performances
Post-Broadway tour (Detroit)

Third-rate hoofer Alfred Lunt goes through his paces as fake countess Lynn Fontanne looks on, in Frank Walts' artwork for this cautionary antiwar comedy-drama from four-time Pulitzer Prize–winner Robert E. Sherwood.

The Pirate 1942
Martin Beck Theatre [Al Hirschfeld] ★ 177 performances

"A frolic, full of extravagant scenery and amusing costumes," said the *Sun* of this Lunt-Fontanne vehicle. "Alfred walks a tightrope, he pulls a rabbit out of a baking dish, turns a pair of gloves into a bouquet, and hypnotizes Lynn." The artwork shows the mountebank Lunt on tightrope, approaching an imperious Fontanne.

The Visit 1958
Lunt-Fontanne Theatre ★ 189 performances
Pre-Broadway tryout (New Haven)

Alfred Lunt and Lynn Fontanne—making their final Broadway appearance as the inaugural attraction at the theatre named in their honor—were "unforgettable," per Brooks Atkinson, in this "bold, grisly drama of negativism and genius."

The Theatre Guild Presents

IDIOT'S DELIGHT

A Play by Robert E. Sherwood

with Alfred & Lynn

LUNT FONTANNE

F. Wales

THE PULITZER PRIZE PLAY of 1936

JOHN GIELGUD AND JUDITH ANDERSON

Come of Age 1934
Maxine Elliott Theatre ★ 35 performances

This striking Judith Anderson vehicle—about a modern-day reincarnation of the poet Thomas Chatterton, who committed suicide in 1770 at the age of seventeen—was billed as "an unusual play," and it certainly was.

Hamlet 1936
Empire Theatre ★ 132 performances
Post-Broadway tour (Boston)

John Gielgud's *Hamlet,* with Judith Anderson as Gertrude (in this photo by Florence Vandamm), bested Edwin Booth's 100 performances and John Barrymore's 101. Richard Burton—directed by Gielgud—set a new record in 1964, with 137.

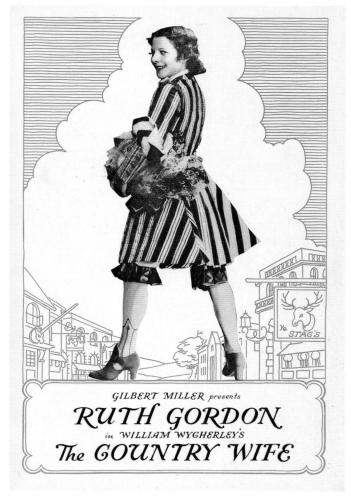

Uncle Vanya 1930
Cort Theatre ★ 96 performances
Post-Broadway tour (Boston)

"Uncle Vanya is the finest of Chekhov's plays," said the
World, "Chekhov's plays are the finest of this century, and Jed
Harris's production is the best Chekhov that America has
seen." Artist Ben Solowey captured Lillian Gish, who, at the
height of her motion picture fame, returned to the stage
as the silent picture era ended.

The Country Wife 1936
Henry Miller's Theatre ★ 89 performances

Ruth Gordon, looking like a lascivious Minnie Mouse, "rouses
the rafters with her uproarious monkeyshines" in William
Wycherley's 1675 comedy. Oliver Messel provided the eye-
catching Restoration garb.

Coquette 1927
Maxine Elliott's Theatre ★ 366 performances
Post-Broadway tour (Boston)

"Helen Hayes gives one of the most resourceful performances of the year," said the *Sun*, "all right, then, of two, five, ten years. What she did with the second act finale was nobody's business but the whole hurrahing theatre's." Hayes, who made her Broadway debut in 1909 at the age of nine, had her first major commercial hit in company with George Abbott and Jed Harris.

Time Remembered 1957
Morosco Theatre ★ 248 performances
Pre-Broadway tryout (Washington)

Helen Hayes, Richard Burton, and Susan Strasberg joined together for this Jean Anouilh fantasy, which Brooks Atkinson found to be "gorgeous theatre all the way through, everything and everyone being just about ideal."

I Am a Camera 1951
Empire Theatre ★ 262 performances
Post-Broadway tour (Washington)

Julie Harris made a striking Sally Bowles and won her first of five Tony Awards in this uneven play, adapted from stories by Christopher Isherwood, which later served as source material for the musical *Cabaret*. This stylish drawing of Bowles-with-cigarette-holder is by Knetson.

Pal Joey 1940
Ethel Barrymore Theatre ★ 374 performances

"A hard-boiled delight, a brilliant, sardonic and strikingly original musical comedy,"
said the *Herald Tribune* of this Rodgers & Hart musical. Newcomer Gene Kelly—
surrounded here by smiling chorus girls—was propelled directly to Hollywood.

The Doctor's Dilemma 1941
Shubert Theatre ★ 121 performances

"In a clairvoyant moment in 1906, Bernard Shaw described Katharine Cornell as she appeared last night at the Shubert," said the *Journal-American*. Cornell, looking radiant in this Marcel Vertès portrait, appeared opposite Raymond Massey.

Set to Music 1939
Music Box Theatre ★ 129 performances

Beatrice Lillie wowed the crowd with "Mad About the Boy," "I'm So Weary of It All," and "I've Been to a Marvelous Party" in this Noël Coward revue recycled from an earlier West End hit. This colorful portrait is by Canadian painter Grant Macdonald.

AL JOLSON

"HOLD ON TO YOUR HATS"

SAM BYRD

presents

PAUL ROBESON

In a New Play with Music

"JOHN HENRY"

by ROARK BRADFORD
and JACQUES WOLFE

Company of 60

Staged by ANTHONY BROWN

Scenery designed by
ALBERT JOHNSON

Choral direction by
LEONARD de PAUR

Hold on to Your Hats 1940
Shubert Theatre ★ 158 performances

"Hold your sides as tightly as the title directs you to hold your hat," said Brooks Atkinson. "Jolson is a little older now, his hair is a little thinner, but none of the warmth has gone out of his singing." The star—whose wife, Ruby Keeler, walked out of the show and the marriage during the tryout—quickly tired and left Broadway forever.

John Henry 1940
44th Street Theatre ★ 7 performances
Pre-Broadway tryout (Boston)

"The rich, eager, laughing, singing, exultant, passionate soul of a race comes alive on the stage," promised the press agent. This Paul Robeson vehicle was scuttled by especially inept material.

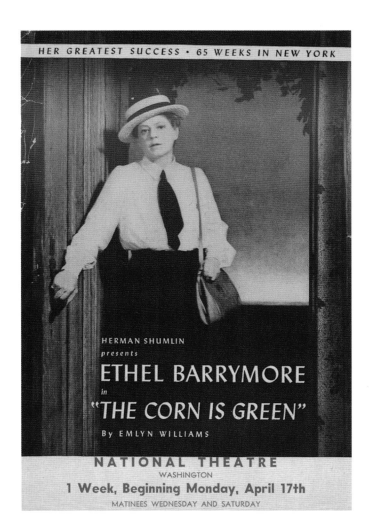

The Corn Is Green 1940
National Theatre [Nederlander] ★ 477 performances
Post-Broadway tour (Washington)

"So happy was the audience over both the good luck of a favorite first lady and the discovery of a good drama, that it remained after the play to ring up fourteen curtain calls, eight of them in honor of Miss Barrymore solo," reported the *Daily News.*

Miss Moffat 1974
Closed out-of-town
Pre-Broadway tryout (Baltimore)

This excessively dreary musicalization of *The Corn Is Green* was shucked when Bette Davis wrenched her back in Philadelphia and called the whole thing off. The investors made out okay, anyway, courtesy of the insurance man.

THE THEATRE GUILD presents

KATHARINE HEPBURN

in

As You Like It

A Comedy by WILLIAM SHAKESPEARE

| William PRINCE | Vanessa BROWN | Milton PARSONS |
| Dudley JONES | Aubrey MATHER | Whitford KANE |

Production Conceived and Directed by
MICHAEL BENTHALL

Scenery and costumes designed by JAMES BAILEY

Production under the supervision of
THERESA HELBURN *and* LAWRENCE LANGNER

BILTMORE THEATRE

LOS ANGELES   MATINEES WEDNESDAY and SATURDAY

2 WEEKS ONLY, BEGINNING MONDAY, DECEMBER 4

PRICES: Eves. — Orch., Boxes and Loges $4.20; 1st Balc. $3.60, $3.00, $2.40; 2nd Balc. $1.80, $1.20
Mats: Orch., Boxes and Loges $3.60; 1st Balc. $3.00, $2.40; 2nd Balc. $1.80, $1.20 (Tax Included)
A THEATRE GUILD-AMERICAN THEATRE SOCIETY SUBSCRIPTION PLAY

Every Sunday Night "THE THEATRE GUILD ON THE AIR" — Station KFI 5:30 to 6:30 P. M.

As You Like It 1950
Cort Theatre ★ 145 performances
Post-Broadway tour (Los Angeles)

Katharine Hepburn "looks like a high-bred swan as the banished daughter of a previously banished Duke," said the *World-Telegram,* adding that "when she dresses as a boy, abbreviated costumes not only make the nickname 'Gams Hepburn' inevitable, but classify the star as a cover girl, full length."

Coco 1969
Mark Hellinger Theatre ★ 329 performances
Post-Broadway tour (Baltimore)

"*Coco* is undoubtedly going to be a big hit," said the *Post*, "but it is a surprisingly dull show, seriously handicapped by an inferior book and a very minor score." Hepburn managed to pull it off, but just barely. The costume and logo is by the production's designer, Cecil Beaton.

A Matter of Gravity 1976
Broadhurst Theatre ★ 79 performances
Pre-Broadway tryout (Washington)

This "contemporary comedy about a sophisticated, vibrant woman with a fine sense of heritage and a deep fascination with life, love and mortality" was a dud, despite the presence of Hepburn and a pre-*Superman* Christopher Reeve.

The Philadelphia Story 1939
Shubert Theatre ★ 417 performances
Pre-Broadway tour (Washington)

"Few actresses of the modern theatre have been mocked and criticized so cruelly and unjustly," said the *Herald Tribune*, "and now Katharine Hepburn turns upon the skeptics and the hecklers and offers one of the most enchanting performances of the season."

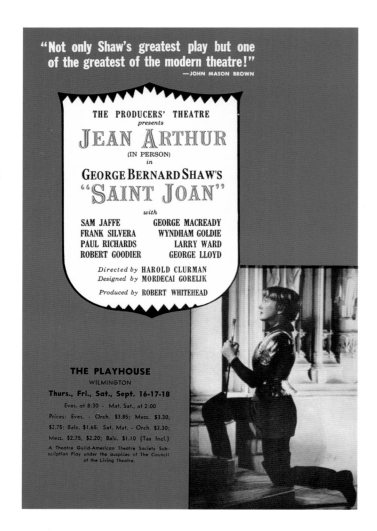

Saint Joan 1954
Closed out-of-town
Pre-Broadway tryout (Wilmington, Delaware)

Hollywood's Jean Arthur attempted a comeback as Shaw's heroine, but—as in *Born Yesterday*—became indisposed and withdrew prior to the Broadway opening.

Saint Joan 1951
Cort Theatre ★ 140 performances
Preliminary credits

Uta Hagen "brings us the first top-flight work of the season and makes the theatre something worth venerating again," said Brooks Atkinson. "In every respect life looks a lot brighter in this neighborhood."

The Lark 1955
Longacre Theatre ★ 229 performances
Pre-Broadway tryout (Boston)

"A beautiful, beautiful play, and in it Julie Harris gives a great performance," said the *Daily News* of Anouilh's retelling of the life of Joan of Arc. "This performance is electrifying, and even now, some hours later, I am still shaken by it."

KERMIT BLOOMGARDEN presents

JULIE HARRIS

as JOAN of ARC in

The LARK

A Play by Jean Anouilh
Adapted by LILLIAN HELLMAN
also STARRING

BORIS KARLOFF

with

JOSEPH WISEMAN • GEOFFREY TOONE • THEODORE BICKEL

Directed by JOSEPH ANTHONY
Light-Setting by JO MIELZINER

Costumes by ALVIN COLT   Music composed by LEONARD BERNSTEIN

PLYMOUTH THEATRE

BOSTON

Friday, Oct. 28 thru Saturday, Nov. 12

MATINEES THURSDAY AND SATURDAY

Evenings — Orch. $4.40; 1st Balc. $3.85, $3.30, $2.75; 2nd Balc. $1.65
Matinees—Orch. $3.85; 1st Balc. $3.30, $2.75, $2.20; 2nd Balc. $1.65 (Tax Included)

Duel of Angels 1960
Helen Hayes Theatre (on 46th Street) ★ 51 performances
Post-Broadway tour (Chicago)

Vivien Leigh, suffering from severe depression and the termination
of her marriage to Laurence Olivier, came to America in Jean
Giraudoux's "striking and provocative" adaptation of *Lucrece*.
Leigh displayed "brilliant irony, ruthlessness and sympathy,"
said the *Post*.

Gigi 1951
Fulton Theatre [Helen Hayes (on 46th Street)] ★ 217 performances
Post-Broadway tour (Pittsburgh)

Twenty-two-year-old Audrey Hepburn—"as fresh and frisky as a
puppy out of a tub," per Walter Kerr—became an overnight star
as Colette's cocotte in this "hilarious and naughty comedy."

ROGER L. STEVENS and S. HUROK
present

VIVIEN LEIGH

in

"DUEL OF ANGELS"

A Play by JEAN GIRAUDOUX

Translated and Adapted by CHRISTOPHER FRY

with

PETER WYNGARDE   JOHN MERIVALE
ALAN MacNAUGHTAN   SALLY HOME

Settings by   Lighting By   Women's Costumes Designed by
ROGER FURSE   PAUL MORRISON   CHRISTIAN DIOR

Directed by ROBERT HELPMANN

BLACKSTONE THEATRE CHICAGO
3 Weeks Only -- September 12 to October 1
Evenings (except Sundays) 8:30 P.M. — Mats. Wed. and Sat. at 2:00 P.M.
EXTRA PERFORMANCE—SUN., SEPT. 25 at 7:00 P.M.   Benefit, Actors' Fund of America
A Theatre Guild-American Theatre Society Subscription Play under the auspices of The Council of the Living Theatre

"*Young Miss Hepburn becomes a star on first U.S. try.*"
—Life Magazine

Star Light! Star Bright!

"Captivating"
—ATKINSON, N. Y. Times

"Simply Grand"
—GARLAND, N. Y. Journal American

"Enchanting"
—WATTS, N. Y. Post

"Beautiful"
—HAWKINS, N. Y. World-Tel. & Sun

"Fresh and Frisky"
—KERR, N. Y. Herald Tribune

"Vital and Warm"
—COLEMAN, N. Y. Daily Mirror

"Charming"
—CHAPMAN, N. Y. Daily News

"*Audrey Hepburn is nearly perfect as 'GIGI' in as engaging a
comedy as we are likely to see for a long time.*"
—GIBBS, The New Yorker

GILBERT MILLER presents

AUDREY
HEPBURN in *Gigi*

A New Comedy by ANITA LOOS adapted from COLETTE'S Novel

NIXON THEATRE
PITTSBURGH
1 WEEK BEGINNING MONDAY OCTOBER 13
MATINEES WEDNESDAY & SATURDAY
PRICES: Evenings - Orchestra $3.90; Mezzanine $3.25; Balcony $2.60, $1.95, $1.30
Matinees - Orchestra $3.25; Mezzanine $2.60; Balcony $1.95, $1.30 (Tax Included)

More Stately Mansions 1967
Broadhurst Theatre ★ 142 performances

One of Eugene O'Neill's final plays, abandoned and unfinished at the time of his death, was unwisely unearthed and resulted in understandable failure. This despite the presence of three Tony Award–winning stars, led by Ingrid Bergman.

There Was a Little Girl 1960
Cort Theatre ★ 16 performances
Pre-Broadway tryout (Boston), preliminary credits

Jane Fonda made her Broadway debut as "a young girl on the brink of womanhood who meets violence by two young men and finds herself rejected by love, society and finally by her own family." Brooks Atkinson found it "adolescent and malodorous." The producers made an interesting choice for their artwork, depicting a character who has been effectively silenced.

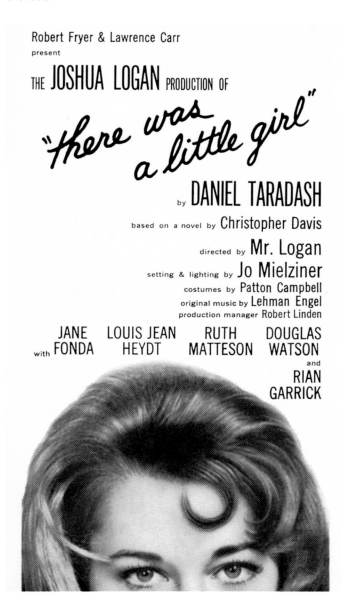

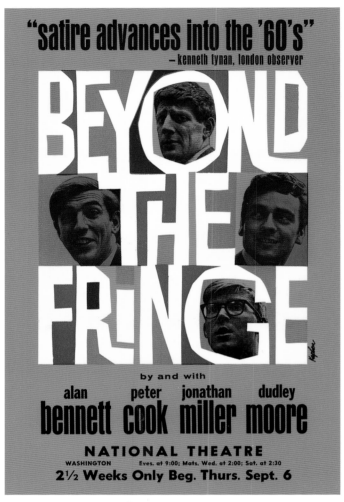

An Evening with Mike Nichols and Elaine May 1960
John Golden Theatre ★ 306 performances

"Merely magnificent," said the *Journal-American.* "A young
man with a bland face and a girl who looks exactly like Anne
Bancroft work on an almost barren stage, and they give you
two hours of as much hilarity as you can endure." Photographer
Richard Avedon perfectly captured this neurotic, odd couple.

Beyond the Fringe 1962
John Golden Theatre ★ 667 performances
Pre-Broadway tryout (Washington)

"With malice toward none, but with surgery for all, they hack
away at every sacred English-speaking institution," said the
World-Telegram. "Never in my life have I laughed so hard."
Actor-writers Alan Bennett, Peter Cook, Jonathan Miller,
and Dudley Moore pioneered a new form of British satire and
each went on to notable careers.

DAVID MERRICK
in association with
JACK ROLLINS and CHARLES JOFFE
presents

WOODY ALLEN
in

PLAY IT AGAIN, SAM

A NEW COMEDY by WOODY ALLEN

Also Starring

ANTHONY ROBERTS

Directed by JOSEPH HARDY

NATIONAL THEATRE
WASHINGTON

Thurs. JAN. 9 thru Sat. JAN. 25

Evenings at 7:30 P.M.   Matinees Wed. and Sat. at 2:00 P.M.

Mon. thru Thurs. Evenings Orch. $6.50; 1st Balc. $6.50, 5.50, 4.50; Upper Balc. $2.25
Fri. and Sat. Evenings Orch. $7.50; 1st Balc. $7.50, 6.50, 5.50; Upper Balc. $3.00
Wed. and Sat. Matinees Orch. $5.50; 1st Balc. $5.50, 4.50, 3.00; Upper Balc. $1.95

Play It Again, Sam 1969
Broadhurst Theatre ★ 453 performances
Pre-Broadway tryout (Washington)

Woody Allen—"the living theatre's most romantic figure," as described by the press agent—
made his only Broadway stage appearance in this comedy that was "convulsingly funny."
The ads warned that "it might be advisable to bring your personal physician with you."
Illustrator Nick Nappi gives us Woody à la Bogey.

GEORGE W. GEORGE & FRANK GRANAT
and
HOWARD ERSKINE   EDWARD SPECTER PRODUCTIONS   PETER S. KATZ
present

SANDY   DON
DENNIS   PORTER

IN THE SMASH COMEDY HIT!

any
WEDNESDAY

by
MURIEL RESNIK

"Delightfully
Wacky
Comedy"
—TIME MAGAZINE

with
ROSEMARY MURPHY
GENE HACKMAN

Scenery Designed by   Lighting by   Costumes by
ROBERT RANDOLPH   THARON MUSSER   THEONI V. ALDREDGE

Directed by
HENRY KAPLAN

MUSIC BOX THEATRE
45th ST. W. of B'WAY   MATS. WED. & SAT.

Any Wednesday 1964
Music Box Theatre ★ 982 performances

"Go, go, go," urged the *World-Telegram* about this sex farce that made a star of Sandy
Dennis and propelled Gene Hackman to Hollywood. The play—which almost folded
during its turmoil-wracked tryout—magically transformed itself into a lucrative moneymaker.

CLAIRE NICHTERN and ZEV BUFMAN
are proud to present

DUSTIN HOFFMAN
In
"JiMMY SHiNE"

A New Play by
MURRAY SCHiSGAL

With (in alphabetical order)

BARBARA CASON   GALE DIXON   DOROTHY EMMERSON
CLEAVON LITTLE   RUE McCLANAHAN   ELI MINTZ   PAMELA PAYTON-WRIGHT
CARLA PINZA   CHARLES SIEBERT   SUSAN SULLIVAN   ARNOLD WILKERSON

Scenery By   Lighting By   Costumes By
EDWARD BURBRIDGE   THOMAS SKELTON   LEWIS BROWN

Music and Lyrics by
JOHN SEBASTIAN

Directed By
DONALD DRiVER

PHOTO CONCEPTION BY EDWARD BURBRIDGE

Jimmy Shine 1968
Brooks Atkinson Theatre ★ 161 performances
Pre-Broadway tryout (Baltimore), preliminary credits

Dustin Hoffman, of *The Graduate,* returned victoriously to Broadway. (Two years earlier he
had been the lowly assistant stage manager and understudy for *The Subject Was Roses*.)
"Mr. Hoffman takes the play, what little there is of it, and waltzes right away with it," said
Clive Barnes in the *Times*. "You are so fascinated with the performance that you scarcely
have time to realize the slender play it is being lavished upon."

A MUST SEE!

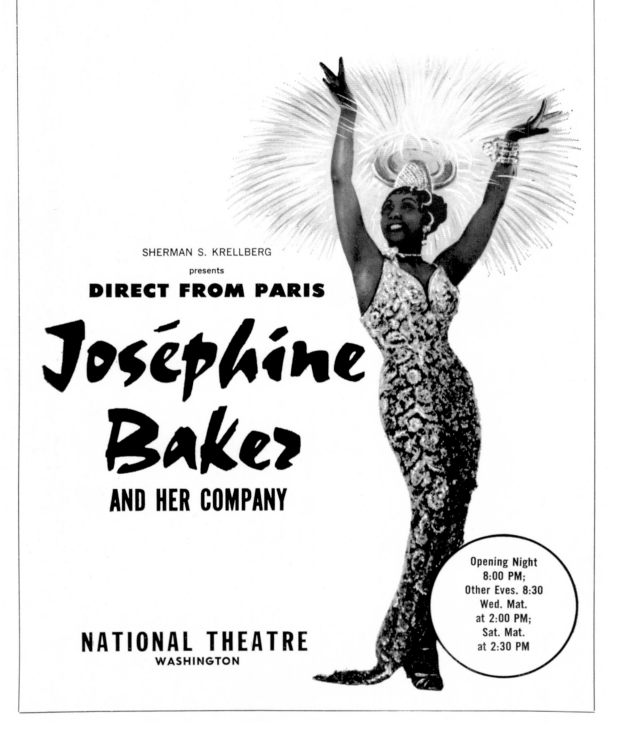

LIMITED ENGAGEMENT!
6 DAYS ONLY — MON. MAR. 16 thru SAT. MAR. 21

SHERMAN S. KRELLBERG
presents
DIRECT FROM PARIS

Joséphine
Baker
AND HER COMPANY

Opening Night
8:00 PM;
Other Eves. 8:30
Wed. Mat.
at 2:00 PM;
Sat. Mat.
at 2:30 PM

NATIONAL THEATRE
WASHINGTON

Josephine Baker 1964
Brooks Atkinson Theatre ★ 40 performances
Post-Broadway tour (Washington)

"Direct from Paris, where she has been adored and feted since she wore a costume of
bananas to introduce the Charleston to the Continent," enthused the press agent, "the
world's best-dressed woman will be singing her love songs in five languages [and]
doing her torrid dances that need no translation."

Catherine Was Great 1944
Alvin Theatre [Neil Simon] ★ 191 performances
Post-Broadway tour

"Mae West returned to Broadway last night, decked out like a battleship in a swimming pool," said the *Herald Tribune.* And this from John Chapman of the *Daily News:* "I am afraid that it will be a bust, which will give Miss West one more than she needs."

It Isn't Working

BROADWAY'S BIGGEST HITS ARE CELEBRATED IN STORY, CHERISHED IN MEMORY, and continually recollected. And revived, too. But there is something intrinsically fascinating about a big Broadway failure.

Broadway shows—musicals, especially—are an intricate mesh of the ideas and talents of a committee of people. Nobody really knows how the material will play until the show, fully assembled, is presented before a paying audience. Any number of plays and musicals have been fixed and doctored on the road; that is the purpose, after all, of pre-Broadway tryouts. But some especially unfortunate shows, once unveiled, proved simply hopeless. The result: a quick and painful trip to the Broadway flophouse.

The pages that follow contain artwork from failures. Some were highly anticipated, with substantial advance-ticket sales; others were hopeless enterprises that simply faded away in a cloud of red ink. Behind each and every one of these shows were high hopes and shattered dreams of writers and performers and producers and investors. Nobody sets out to do a stinker. And nobody, not even major stars or major players, is immune—as is evidenced by the parade of top box-office names represented.

Lyn Austin and Thomas Noyes
present

NANCY WALKER
in the new musical comedy
"COPPER and BRASS"

also starring
JOAN BLONDELL

with

DICK WILLIAMS   ALICE PEARCE   ALAN BUNCE
Norma Douglas   Peter Conlow

Book by **ELLEN VIOLETT** and **DAVID CRAIG**
Music by **DAVID BAKER**
Lyrics by **DAVID CRAIG**
Directed by **MARC DANIELS**
Dances and Musical Numbers by **ANNA SOKOLOW**
Settings and Lighting by **WILLIAM** and **JEAN ECKART**
Costumes by **ALVIN COLT**

Orchestrations by
Ralph Burns

Musical Direction and Vocal Arrangements by
Maurice Levine

Dance Arrangements by
John Morris

SHUBERT THEATRE
NEW HAVEN
Fri. Eve., Sept. 13 thru Sat. Eve., Sept. 21
MATINEES WEDNESDAY AND SATURDAY

Copper and Brass 1957
Martin Beck Theatre [Al Hirschfeld] ★ 36 performances
Pre-Broadway tryout (New Haven), preliminary credits

Nancy Walker played a policewoman "who blows her whistle
for a jazzband leader" in what Brooks Atkinson called a
"standard, old-fashioned show with a breathlessly unfunny
book, uninteresting music, unlovely ballets and a general look
of banality." Al Hirschfeld, naturally enough, put his lady copper
on a brass sax.

Fade Out—Fade In 1964
Mark Hellinger Theatre ★ 199 performances
Pre-Broadway tryout (Boston)

Al Hirschfeld captured budding star Carol Burnett who
headlined "Broadway's biggest and most generous and most
welcome gift to the World's Fair multitudes" (per press agent
Harvey Sabinson). The show faded out in a flurry of lawsuits
when Burnett became indisposed.

**Wednesday, April 29
thru
Saturday, May 16**

Matinees Wednesday and Saturday
Matinees 1st week
Thurs. & Sat., 2nd
& 3rd Weeks Wed. & Sat.

LESTER OSTERMAN and JULE STYNE
present

CAROL BURNETT

in

FADE OUT FADE IN

A New Musical Comedy

Book and Lyrics by **BETTY COMDEN & ADOLPH GREEN**

Music by **JULE STYNE**

Also Starring

JACK CASSIDY

with

DICK PATTERSON
REUBEN SINGER

TINA LOUISE
VIRGINIA PAYNE

MITCHELL JASON
TIGER HAYNES

and

LOU JACOBI

Dances and Musical Numbers Staged by **ERNEST FLATT**

Settings and Lighting by
WILLIAM & JEAN ECKART

Hair Styles by
ERNEST ADLER

Costumes by
DONALD BROOKS

Musical Direction
COLIN ROMOFF

Orchestrations by
RALPH BURNS & RAY ELLIS

Vocal Arrangements by
BUSTER DAVIS

Dance Music Arranged by
RICHARD DE BENEDICTIS

Directed by **GEORGE ABBOTT**

Original Cast Album on ABC-Paramount Records
An ABC-Paramount—On-Stage Recording

COLONIAL THEATRE

BOSTON

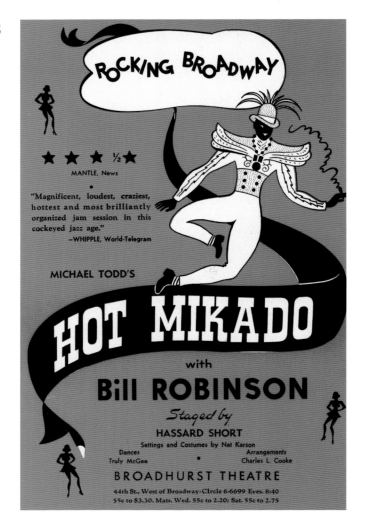

Hot Mikado 1939
Broadhurst Theatre ★ 85 performances

When producer Mike Todd was unable to obtain the transfer rights to the W.P.A.'s all-Negro *Swing Mikado,* he decided to produce his own swing version of the Gilbert & Sullivan operetta (starring the great Bill Robinson as a tap-dancing Lord High Executioner). Both *Mikado*s opened on Broadway within a month, to quick failure.

Mata Hari 1967
Closed out-of-town
Pre-Broadway tryout (Washington)

"The night was so bad, there was no curtain call and the audience left," reported *Variety* from the Washington premiere of this legendary Vincente Minnelli failure. Leading lady Marisa Mell, shot dead by the firing squad, visibly rubbed her nose as the curtain fell.

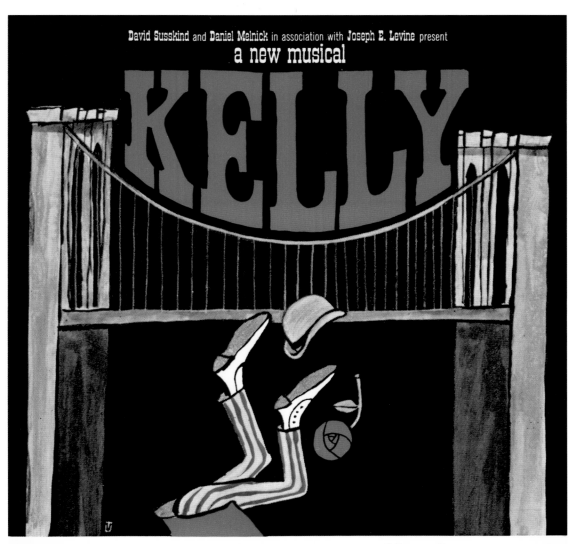

Kelly 1965
Broadhurst Theatre ★ 1 performance
Pre-Broadway tryout (Philadelphia), preliminary credits

Kelly, about Steve Brodie, a ne'er-do-well who survived a (purported) jump off the Brooklyn Bridge in 1886, stunned the entertainment world as the first big-budget Broadway musical to close on opening night. The loss was an astounding $650,000, at a time when you could produce shows like *Hello, Dolly!* or *Fiddler on the Roof* for under $400,000. Illustrator Tomi Ungerer showed the hero—with derby and rose—plunging into the East River.

The Man Who Came to Dinner 1939
Music Box Theatre ★ 739 performances

The viperish Sheridan Whiteside—surrounded by penguins and other useless Christmas gifts—is served up on a plate. "An evening of astringent merry-making," said Brooks Atkinson, "it is American in its comic tone, Broadway in craftsmanship, and a roaring evening of literate hilarity." Things didn't work so well with the musical version . . .

Sherry! 1967
Alvin Theatre [Neil Simon] ★ 72 performances
Pre-Broadway tryout (Philadelphia), preliminary credits

"Perfectly awful," said Martin Gottfried in *Women's Wear Daily.* "An aimless, disorganized shadow of a dated comedy with aimless, disorganized songs and dances tacked onto it with no sense of musical theatre." George Sanders—shown here in this artwork from *Mad* magazine's Jack Davis—was replaced on the road, along with the director.

We Take the Town 1962
Closed out-of-town

Robert Preston (fourth from the right in this rendition by Oscar Liebman), just off *The Music Man,* struck out as the legendary Mexican bandit Pancho Villa.

STUART OSTROW presents

ROBERT PRESTON
as PANCHO VILLA

in
WE TAKE THE TOWN
A Musical Adventure

Lyrics by MATT DUBEY
Music by HAROLD KARR
Book by FELICE BAUER & MATT DUBEY
Choreography by DONALD SADDLER

with
MIKE KELLIN   JOHN CULLUM   CARMEN ALVAREZ   KATHLEEN WIDDOES   ROMNEY BRENT   LESTER RAWLINS

Settings by PETER LARKIN
Costumes by MOTLEY
Musical & Vocal Direction by COLIN ROMOFF
Orchestrations by ROBERT RUSSELL BENNETT & HERSHY KAY
ORIGINAL CAST ALBUM BY COLUMBIA RECORDS

Production Directed by ALEX SEGAL

Opens Thursday, April 5th
BROADWAY THEATRE

Broadway at 53rd Street   -:-   Mats. Wed. and Sat.

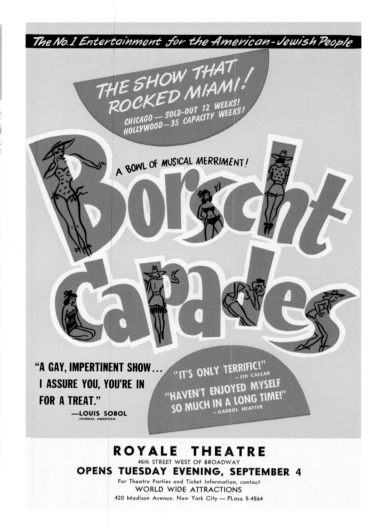

Kosher Kitty Kelly 1925
Times Square Theatre ★ 105 performances

This knockoff of the long-running 1922 hit comedy *Abie's Irish Rose* was touted by the producers as a "delightful story of the East Side of New York, with its quaint romance and foreign-tinged life."

Borscht Capades 1951
Royale Theatre ★ 90 performances

An "American entertainment aimed at American-Jewish theater-goers in New York who don't like to stray away from Broadway," this offering was headlined by the clarinet-playing Mickey Katz. Featured in the cast was the star's nineteen-year-old son Joel Kaye (né Joel Katz, now Joel Grey).

KEN GASTON and LEONARD GOLDBERG
in association with HENRY STERN
present

LEON URIS'
ARI

A New Musical Based on his Novel

EXODUS

Book and Lyrics by
LEON URIS

Music by
WALT SMITH

Starring

DAVID CRYER · CONSTANCE TOWERS

Also Starring

MARTIN ROSS · C. K. ALEXANDER

NORWOOD SMITH · MARK ZELLER · JACK GWILLIM

JAMIE ROSS · JOSEPH DELLA SORTE

and

JOHN SAVAGE · JACQUELINE MAYRO
as Dov   as Karen

Scenery Designed by
ROBERT RANDOLPH

Costumes by
SARA BROOK

Lighting by
NANANNE PORCHER

Vocal Arrangements &
Musical Direction by
STANLEY LEBOWSKY

Orchestrations by
PHILIP J. LANG

Dance & Incidental Music
Arranged by
PETER HOWARD

Production Stage Manager: WADE MILLER

Associate Producers: RONALD RECKSEIT, LISA LIPSKY

Choreography by
TALLEY BEATTY

Production Directed by
LUCIA VICTOR

Original Cast Recording by

Ari 1971
Mark Hellinger Theatre ★ 19 performances
Pre-Broadway tryout (Washington)

This song-and-dance version of Leon Uris's novel *Exodus*—featuring book and lyrics by
Broadway-novice Uris himself, as well as a concentration camp ballet—was predictably
inept and quickly laughed off the stage.

Reuben Reuben 1955
Closed out-of-town
Pre-Broadway tryout (Boston)

This incomprehensible tale of a manic-depressive acrobat by the wildly creative Marc Blitzstein was hailed by the critic of the *Boston Herald* as "one of the most bewildering evenings I have ever spent in the theatre."

The Pink Jungle 1959
Closed out-of-town
Pre-Broadway tryout (Boston)

"One has the uneasy feeling that one has been through it all before, possibly in high school," said the *Detroit Free Press* of this musical about the cosmetics world, with Ginger Rogers attempting to jump-start her post-Hollywood career. Tom Morrow's "lovely with makeup mirror" was *not* meant to represent Ginger.

L. SLADE BROWN presents

EDDIE **FOY** KAYE **BALLARD**

in a new musical

ROYAL FLUSH

Also Starring

KENNETH NELSON

LOUIS EDMONDS DICK O'NEILL JILL O'HARA CHARLOTTE JONES BERNIE MEYER

and

JANE CONNELL BEVERLY TODD

Book, Music & Lyrics by JAY THOMPSON

Sets and Costumes Designed by RAOUL PENE DU BOIS

Lighting Designed by JULES FISHER

Musical Direction by SKIP REDWINE Orchestrations by LARRY WILCOX Dance Music Arranged by HAL SCHAEFER Based on "The Green Bird" by NINA SAVO

Directed and Choreographed by JACK COLE

SHUBERT THEATRE
PHILADELPHIA

**TUES., JAN. 19
thru SAT., FEB. 6**

Royal Flush 1964
Closed out-of-town
Pre-Broadway tryout (Philadelphia), preliminary credits

This misguided musical—about a queen imprisoned in an underground bathroom
(hence the title)—quickly went down the toilet in Philadelphia, despite the
replacement of the star and director-choreographer. Artist Nick Nappi presents
us with a not-so-royal monarch. *The Green Bird,* Julie Taymor's 2000 adaptation
of the same source material, proved similarly unworkable.

The Girl from Nantucket 1945
Adelphi Theatre [George Abbott] ★ 12 performances
Pre-Broadway tryout (Philadelphia)

"The new musical takes a bad book, dresses it up with wheezy gags, sets it to very ordinary music and lyrics, and tosses in a weirdly dull ballet about a Whale and a Fisherman fighting for the caresses of the Sea," reported the *Herald Tribune*. The artwork was contributed by the costume designer, Lou Eisele.

Pleasure Dome 1955
Closed in rehearsals
Pre-Broadway tryout (Washington)

"A Cook's tour of the Palaces of Mirth and a sightseer's delight, a mecca of merriment" is how the press agent described this revue. It closed in rehearsals, without ever hitting the stage.

Nice Goin'! 1939
Closed out-of-town
Pre-Broadway tryout (Boston)

This musical quickly folded despite "girls you love to look at," a score from Hollywood's Ralph Rainger and Leo Robin (Oscar winners for "Thanks for the Memory"), and Mary Martin in her first starring role. The artwork, one supposes, is meant to be suggestive.

HENRY ADRIAN
presents
JAMES BARTON
in a Whale of a Show

The Girl from Nantucket

A Modern Musical Comedy

LOU EISELE

with **JACK DURANT**

EVELYN WYCKOFF   **HELEN RAYMOND**

JANE KEAN   **BOB KENNEDY**

Kim and Kathy Gaynes—Tom Ladd—Marion Niles
And A Breezy Cast of 80

tony curtis
in
**the
one-night
stand**
A New Comedy by
Bruce Jay Friedman and **Jacques Levy**
with
William Devane
Directed by
Mr. Levy and **Mr. Friedman**
SHUBERT THEATRE, *Boston*
SEPTEMBER 24 THRU OCTOBER 6
Evenings at 7:30 -:- Matinees Thurs. and Sat. at 2:00

Soupy Comes To Broadway!

(Note change of
Previews and
opening date)

**SOUPY
SALES**
in
"COME
LIVE
WITH ME"

A NEW COMEDY

Previews Eve. Jan. 17, 18; Mat. Jan. 18
Opens Thurs. Jan. 19

Previews Jan. 10 thru 15 • Opens Mon. Jan. 16

BILLY ROSE THEATRE
208 WEST 41 STREET
MATS. WED. AND SAT.

The One-Night Stand 1973
Closed out-of-town
Pre-Broadway tryout (Boston)

Producer David Merrick removed his name from this "boy meets boy meets girl" stinker in Philly, ultimately deciding to close the show before it reached Boston.

Come Live with Me 1967
Billy Rose Theatre [Nederlander] ★ 4 performances

Pie-in-the-face TV comic Soupy Sales "neither threw nor caught any pies," reported the *Post,* "and that may have been one of the things his frail little vehicle could have done with in its time of sore need." The artwork looks kind of pathetic, doesn't it?

The Master of Thornfield [Jane Eyre] 1958
Belasco Theatre ★ 52 performances
Pre-Broadway tryout (Boston), preliminary credits

The "dashing, reckless, glamorous and phenomenally popular" Errol Flynn was no longer the Master of Thornfield by the time this vanity production reached Broadway. Supermarket heir Huntington Hartford's play arrived with a new star (Eric Portman), a new director, and an old title.

I'm with You 1960
Closed out-of-town
Pre-Broadway tryout (San Francisco)

"'A show like no other' is the way theatre experts prefer to describe *I'm with You,*" said the press agent of Nat King Cole's self-produced attempt to storm Broadway. The ill-assembled enterprise, derived from Cole's concept album *Wild Is Love,* was quickly disbanded.

Alice 1978
Closed out-of-town
Pre-Broadway tryout (Philadelphia)

Producer Mike Nichols attempted to follow up his musical smash *Annie* with this disco version of *Alice,* which shuttered in Philly. That's the up-and-coming Debbie Allen struggling through the looking glass.

Flora, the Red Menace 1965
Alvin Theatre [Neil Simon] ★ 87 performances

"Liza Minnelli, who looks like a charming little rabbit designed by Walt Disney to look like Judy Garland, her mother, is a big new star on Broadway today," said the *Journal-American* of this ill-fitting failure that introduced Minnelli and the songwriting team of John Kander & Fred Ebb. The artwork was ultimately changed, but inserting a bomb in the title treatment was, on consideration, unwise.

COURTNEY BURR
in association with
The Sterling Productions
presents

IN PERSON

ERROL FLYNN

The Master of Thornfield

A Romantic Drama By **HUNTINGTON HARTFORD**
ALSO STARRED

BLANCHE YURKA

Introducing **JAN BROOKS** *as Jane Eyre*

AVIS	NORAH	FRANCIS	JANE	DOUGLAS	CLAUDIA	LORD	ADELAIDE
SCOTT	HOWARD	COMPTON	WHITE	WOOD	CRAWFORD	FOLEY	KLEIN

and

DAVID J. STEWART

Adapted from the novel, "JANE EYRE" by CHARLOTTE BRONTE
Scenery Designed by **BEN EDWARDS** Costumes by **MOTLEY** Incidental Music by **WILL LORIN**

Production
Directed by **PETER ASHMORE**

COLONIAL THEATRE BOSTON
2 Weeks Beginning Tuesday, February 25

MATINEES WEDNESDAY and SATURDAY
Mon. thru Thurs. Eves.—Orch. $4.40; Balc. $3.85, $3.30, $2.75; 2nd Balc. $2.20, $1.65
Fri. and Sat. Eves.—Orch. $4.95; Balc. $3.85, $3.30, $2.75; 2nd Balc. $2.20, $1.65
All Matinees—Orch. $3.85; Balc. $3.30, $2.75, $2.20; 2nd Balc. $1.65, $1.10 (Tax Incl.)

NAT KING COLE

in

I'm With You

a new musical
COMPANY OF 40

BARBARA McNAIR

Lyrics by	Music by	Additional material by
DOTTY WAYNE	RAY RASCH	TOM CLAPP

Production designed by
JIM TRITTIPO
Orchestral, choral arrangements and musical direction by
RALPH CARMICHAEL

Choreography by **EUGENE LORING**

Production directed by **BILL COLLERAN**

Original Cast Album by Capitol Records

GEARY THEATRE
ORdway 3-6440 -:- Geary and Mason Sts.
2 Weeks Beginning Monday, October 31st

Mon. thru Sat. 8:30 P.M. -:- Mats. Wed. and Sat. 2:30 P.M.

WORLD PREMIERE!

MIKE NICHOLS & LEWIS ALLEN PRESENT

ALICE

A NEW MUSICAL
ADAPTED BY VINNETTE CARROLL
FROM THE WORKS OF LEWIS CARROLL

MUSIC & LYRICS BY **MICKI GRANT** CHOREOGRAPHY **TALLEY BEATTY**
ENTIRE PRODUCTION CONCEIVED AND DIRECTED BY **VINNETTE CARROLL**

PRESENTED IN CONJUNCTION WITH **URBAN ARTS CORPS & ANITA McSHANE**

FORREST THEATER

PREVIEWS MAY 23—MAY 30

LIMITED ENGAGEMENT • OPENS TUES., MAY 31

HAROLD PRINCE
presents
A NEW MUSICAL COMEDY

"FLORA, THE RED MENACE"

Based on the novel "Love is Just Around the Corner" by LESTER ATWELL

with

LIZA MINNELLI

MARY LOUISE WILSON **CATHRYN DAMON** **ROBERT KAYE**

STEPHANIE HILL JAMES CRESSON DORTHA DUCKWORTH

JOE E. MARKS LOUIS GUSS

and **BOB DISHY**

Book by
GEORGE ABBOTT and **ROBERT RUSSELL**

Music by	Lyrics by
JOHN KANDER	**FRED EBB**

Dances and Musical Numbers staged by **LEE THEODORE**

Settings by	Costumes by	Lighting by
William and Jean Eckart	**Donald Brooks**	**Tharon Musser**

Musical Direction by	Orchestrations by	Dance Arrangements by
Hal Hastings	**Don Walker**	**David Baker**

Original Cast Album — RCA Victor

Production Directed by **GEORGE ABBOTT**

ALVIN THEATRE
52nd ST. WEST of BROADWAY

Opens Tues. Eve. May 11

Matinees Wednesday and Saturday

Previews Wednesday, May 5 thru Monday, May 10

114

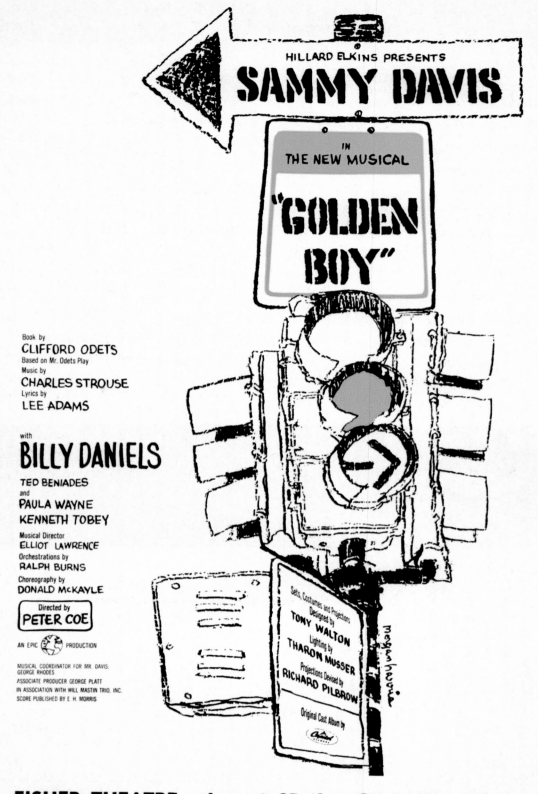

HILLARD ELKINS PRESENTS

SAMMY DAVIS

IN
THE NEW MUSICAL

"GOLDEN BOY"

Book by
CLIFFORD ODETS
Based on Mr. Odets Play
Music by
CHARLES STROUSE
Lyrics by
LEE ADAMS

with
BILLY DANIELS

TED BENIADES
and
PAULA WAYNE
KENNETH TOBEY

Musical Director
ELLIOT LAWRENCE
Orchestrations by
RALPH BURNS
Choreography by
DONALD McKAYLE

Directed by
PETER COE

AN EPIC 🌐 PRODUCTION

MUSICAL COORDINATOR FOR MR. DAVIS:
GEORGE RHODES
ASSOCIATE PRODUCER GEORGE PLATT
IN ASSOCIATION WITH WILL MASTIN TRIO, INC.
SCORE PUBLISHED BY E. H. MORRIS

Sets, Costumes and Projections
Designed by
TONY WALTON
Lighting by
THARON MUSSER
Projections Devised by
RICHARD PILBROW

Original Cast Album by
Capitol

FISHER THEATRE · August 25 thru September 19
DETROIT -:-   Mats. Wed. and Sat. (No Perf. Tues. Eve., Sept. 15 and Wed. Mat., Sept. 16)
EXTRA PERF. SUN. MAT. AND EVE., SEPT. 13

Golden Boy 1964
Majestic Theatre ★ 560 performances
Pre-Broadway tryout (Detroit), preliminary credits

This Sammy Davis vehicle gained a new librettist and a new director on the
road and underwent countless changes, including at least four different pieces
of artwork replacing the original design by Morgan Harris.

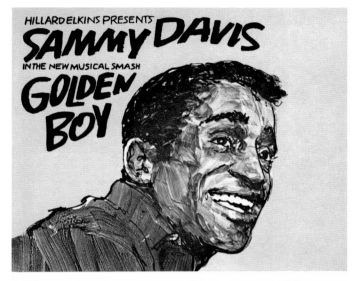

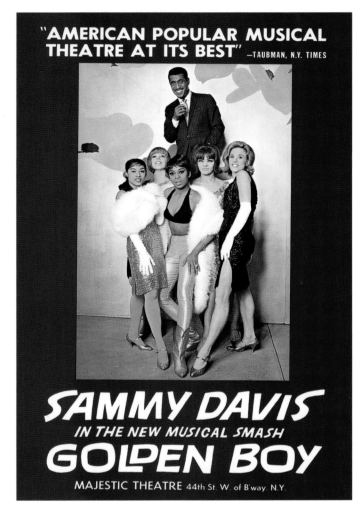

Golden Boy 1964
Majestic Theatre ★ 560 performances

"For the first five minutes of the musical there is every reason to expect something triumphant," said the *World-Telegram,* "you find yourself thinking, if only they can sustain it at this level. . . . they can't." The show opened in New York using this portrait of the star.

Golden Boy 1964
Majestic Theatre ★ 560 performances

In another attempt to sell this problematic musical, they surrounded the star with chorus girls (including Baayork Lee, far left, and Lola Falana, center). *Golden Boy* entered the record book as the first Broadway show to exceed 550 performances and *still* lose money.

Court Square Theatre Springfield · 3 Nights BEG. THURS. April 9

MATINEE SATURDAY   A PLAYGOERS ATTRACTION

BEN TOMKINS and ALVIN COOPERMAN
present

THE NEW COMEDY

Masquerade

by L. S. BIRCHARD and JEROAM STAGG
Starring (IN PERSON)

VERONICA LAKE & CHARLES KORVIN

with LISA FERRADAY

Directed by JOHN LARSON

Scenery & Costumes by JOHN BLANKENCHIP

EUGENE PAUL and WILLIAM I. KAUFMAN
with BLAIR WALLISER
present

"THE PINK ELEPHANT"

A New Comedy by JOHN FULLER

WITH

STEVE ALLEN

Howard Smith · Jean Casto
Bruce Gordon

Directed by HARRY ELLERBE
Settings and Lighting by Ralph Alswang
Costumes by Guy Kent

FORREST THEATRE
PHILADELPHIA
1 Week Only Beg. Tues. Eve., April 7
MATINEES WEDNESDAY, FRIDAY & SATURDAY
PRICES: Evenings - Orch. $3.90; Mezz. $3.25; Balc. $2.60, $1.95, $1.30
Matinees - Orch. $3.25; Mezz. $3.25; Balc. $2.60, $1.95, $1.30 (All Taxes Included)

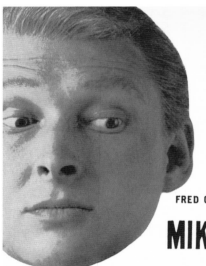

*A New Play
from the producers of*
"TWO FOR THE SEESAW"
"THE MIRACLE WORKER"
"THE TENTH MAN"
"ALL THE WAY HOME"
"GIDEON"
and "A THOUSAND CLOWNS"

FRED COE and ARTHUR CANTOR
present

MIKE NICHOLS
in

ELAINE MAY's
New Comedy

"A MATTER OF POSITION"

Directed by FRED COE

Sets and Lighting by   Costumes by
DAVID HAYS   RUTH MORLEY

Opens Thursday, October 25th

BOOTH THEATRE
45th Street West of Broadway

Eves. at 8:30 -:- Mats. Wed. at 2:00 and Sat. at 2:30

Masquerade 1953
Closed out-of-town
Pre-Broadway tryout (Springfield, Massachusetts)

Hollywood's Veronica Lake starred in this clunker about a penniless waif who hooks up with a romantic jewel thief. "A vivid theatrical experience which keeps audiences on the edge of their seats," promised the press agent, but it nevertheless expired in three weeks.

The Pink Elephant 1953
Playhouse Theatre ★ 5 performances
Pre-Broadway tryout (Philadelphia)

Steve Allen made his only Broadway appearance as a political consultant to a Republican candidate in this dimwitted farce that the *Post* called "terrible," "hopeless," and "repulsive." Twelve weeks after the play closed, Allen went on local TV with a forty-minute late-night talk show that became *The Tonight Show*.

A Matter of Position 1962
Closed out-of-town

The celebrated comedy team of Nichols & May split up after this debacle shuttered in Philadelphia. A revised version was mounted in 2000 under the title *Taller than a Dwarf*, with similar results.

The Tumbler 1960
Helen Hayes Theatre ★ 5 performances

"A dismaying mixture of overheated writing and bad acting," said the *Daily News,* adding that "at the final curtain Heston was getting ready to hang himself in the barn. I hope he didn't really go and do it, because *The Tumbler* is by no means his fault alone."

Face of a Hero 1960
Eugene O'Neill Theatre ★ 36 performances

"Egg splatters the *Face of a Hero*, which opened last night," said the *Times* of this Jack Lemmon vehicle. "Some was flung by intent; a great deal more landed inadvertently, thanks to the ineptitude of the playwright."

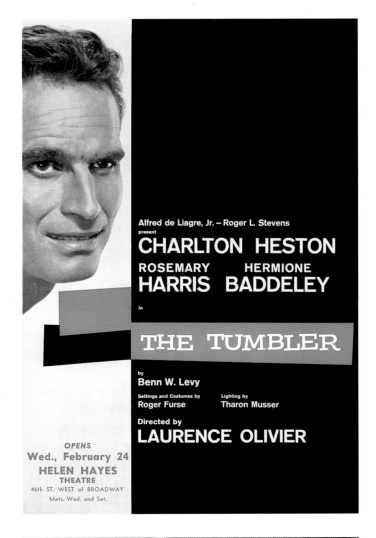

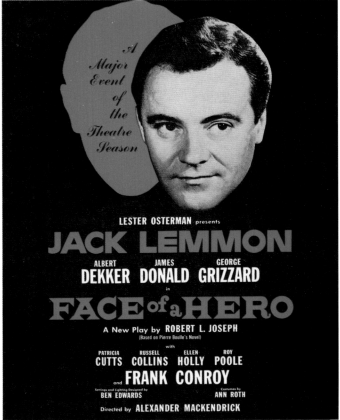

RICHARD KILEY LESLIE UGGAMS

in The New Musical

HER FIRST ROMAN

Based on Bernard Shaw's Caesar & Cleopatra

Her First Roman 1968
Lunt-Fontanne Theatre ★ 17 performances

"The authors made such obvious mistakes," said Walter Kerr, "that a good half of the audience could have stood up, said where and when, and pointed out to the management the rearranged road to happiness." The figures in John Fehnie's artwork decidedly did not resemble stars Richard Kiley and Leslie Uggams.

What Makes Sammy Run? 1964
54th Street Theatre [George Abbott] ★ 540 performances

"*What Makes Sammy Run?* runs backward" headlined the *Daily News* review of this clumsy musical, buoyed by an impressive performance by Steve Lawrence. Oscar Liebman's artwork shows Hollywood producer Sammy Glick—with an oversized cigar—all but devoured by an oversized showgirl.

The Red Shoes 1993
Gershwin Theatre ★ 5 performances

A turmoil-wracked disaster, intended—per the press agent—"for girls everywhere, their mothers, their grandmothers, and all the men who love them." The artwork was far more stylish than the show, which proved to be veteran composer Jule Styne's final work.

Legends! 1986
Closed out-of-town
Pre-Broadway tryout (Washington)

"A back-stabbing, up-staging, tongue-lashing tour de force that really puts a warm glow—along with a little love—back into show business," said the press agent. The stylish artwork by Ken Eula featured two legends, neither of whom looked remotely like stars Mary Martin and Carol Channing.

AHMET M. ERTEGUN KEVIN EGGERS ROBERT REGESTER for EEE Ventures Ltd.

CHERYL CRAWFORD PACE THEATRICAL GROUP

present

MARY MARTIN   CAROL CHANNING

in

Legends!

A New Comedy by
JAMES KIRKWOOD

with

GARY BEACH   ANNIE-JOE

Scenery Designed by	Costumes Designed by	Lighting Designed by
DOUGLAS SCHMIDT	**FREDDY WITTOP**	**THOMAS SKELTON**

Directed by
CLIFFORD WILLIAMS

HAROLD FIELDING
presents
JOE LAYTON'S
Spectacular
Production of
Margaret Mitchell's

NOW
AS AN
EXCITING
STAGE
MUSICAL!

Gone
with the
Wind

Music & Lyrics
HAROLD ROME
Book
HORTON FOOTE

Gone with the Wind 1973
Closed out-of-town
Pre-Broadway tryout (Los Angeles)

Broadway's penchant for surefire, big-budget, screen-to-stage fiascos found one of its most famous victims in Hollywood's biggest motion picture hit ever (at the time), with Lesley Ann Warren as Scarlett and Pernell Roberts as Rhett.

THERE'S NEVER BEEN A MUSICAL LIKE HER.

Carrie

J THE VIRGINIA THEATRE
245 WEST 52nd STREET

AFTER CAPTIVATING MILLIONS OF READERS AND MOVIEGOERS, STEPHEN KING'S MODERN MASTERPIECE IS ABOUT TO TAKE BROADWAY'S BREATH AWAY. CARRIE, THE INTERNATIONAL BEST-SELLING NOVEL AND SMASH-HIT FILM, IS NOW A SPECTACULAR MUSICAL, AND THE GIRL WITH THE UNUSUAL TALENT WILL ENCHANT YOU AS NEVER BEFORE.

THE FRIEDRICH KURZ RSC PRODUCTION

BETTY BUCKLEY IN CARRIE THE MUSICAL BASED ON THE NOVEL BY STEPHEN KING · MUSIC BY MICHAEL GORE · LYRICS BY DEAN PITCHFORD · BOOK BY LAWRENCE D. COHEN · WITH DARLENE LOVE · GENE ANTHONY RAY · CHARLOTTE d'AMBOISE · PAUL GYNGELL · SALLY ANN TRIPLETT · AND INTRODUCING LINZI HATELEY AS CARRIE · MUSIC SUPERVISOR HAROLD WHEELER · MUSICAL DIRECTOR PAUL SCHWARTZ · CHOREOGRAPHER DEBBIE ALLEN · DIRECTOR TERRY HANDS

CALL TELETRON: (212) 246-0102 24 HOURS A DAY/7 DAYS A WEEK GROUP SALES: (212) 398-8383 ALSO AT TICKETRON

J THE VIRGINIA THEATRE 245 WEST 52nd STREET

Carrie 1988
Virginia Theatre ★ 5 performances

"There's never been a musical like her," indeed . . .

Pretty Little Picture

BROADWAY ARTWORK IS DESIGNED, SPECIFICALLY, TO HELP PROMOTE the show in question. Artwork might reflect the material, or the theme, or the performers. Often, the design draws on a combination of elements. The following pages display art for art's sake; that is, artwork that is arresting in itself. Some of these shows had far more to offer than just their artwork; others all too obviously didn't and are long forgotten. But the artwork, for assorted reasons, remains interesting and intriguing.

The reader will recognize the style of a number of the artists whose work appears in this book, with the celebrated Al Hirschfeld in the forefront. Don Freeman, Hilary Knight, and Tom Morrow were frequent and popular Broadway illustrators. A sizable contingent of cartoonists is represented, including a group from the *New Yorker:* James Thurber, John Held Jr., Charles Addams, Ludwig Bemelmans, William Steig, and Peter Arno. (The *New Yorker* was based, conveniently, just down the street from the Broadway ad agencies.) Other illustrators ranged from pinup artist Alberto Vargas to the elegant Marcel Vertès, from Jack Davis of *Mad* magazine to Norman Rockwell of the *Saturday Evening Post.*

Special note should be made of a handful of designs. The artwork for *How to Succeed in Business without Really Trying, Fiorello!, Equus,* and *Dancin'* are among Broadway's best ever. Intriguing and inviting, the art (and the show's title), once seen, remains firmly embedded in memory.

ROBERT E. GRIFFITH and HAROLD S. PRINCE

present

Fiorello!

A New Musical

Book by **JEROME WEIDMAN** and **GEORGE ABBOTT**

Music by **JERRY BOCK**

Lyrics by **SHELDON HARNICK**

with

TOM BOSLEY   PATRICIA WILSON   ELLEN HANLEY   HOWARD DA SILVA

MARK DAWSON   NATHANIEL FREY

and PAT STANLEY

Directed by **GEORGE ABBOTT**

Choreography by **PETER GENNARO**

Scenery & Costumes Designed by **WILLIAM** and **JEAN ECKART**

Musical Direction **HAL HASTINGS**   Orchestrations by **IRWIN KOSTAL**   Dance Music Arranged by **JACK ELLIOTT**

BROADHURST THEATRE

44th STREET WEST OF BROADWAY

Opens Monday, November 23

Matinees Wednesday and Saturday

Fiorello! 1959

Broadhurst Theatre ★ 795 performances

"Fiorello! scored a smashing victory at the polls with humor, heart and zest," said the *Mirror,* "it's a box office landslide, a top ticket for the amusement vote." Fay Gage's silhouette of Mayor Fiorello H. La Guardia—New York's "Little Flower," who left office in 1945—was instantly recognizable.

How to Succeed in Business without Really Trying 1961
46th Street Theatre [Richard Rodgers] ★ 1,417 performances
National tour (Washington)

"Crafty, conniving, sneaky, cynical, irreverent, impertinent, sly, malicious, and lovely, just lovely," said Walter Kerr of this Pulitzer Prize–winning Frank Loesser–Abe Burrows satire on big business. The striking logo, which perfectly captured the authors' tone, is unforgettable.

©1962 (renewed) The Frank Loesser Literary and Musical Trust. Used by permission.

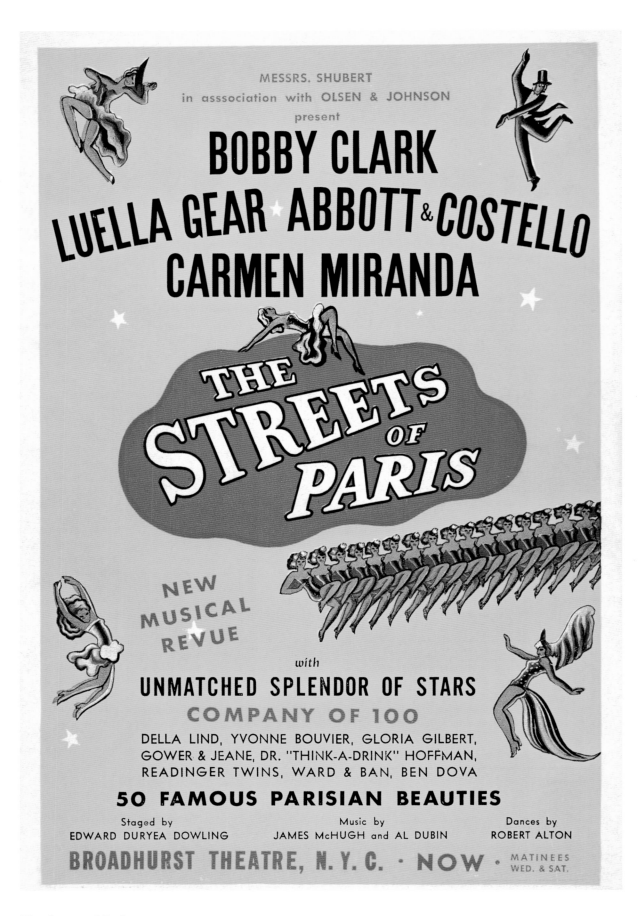

The Streets of Paris 1939
Broadhurst Theatre ★ 274 performances

"Hilarious rowdy-dow," said the *World-Telegram,* "slam-bang, poke-in-the-nose comedy that hypnotizes an entire audience into delirium." This revue top-lined comedian Bobby Clark while introducing newcomers Carmen Miranda, Abbott and Costello, and Gower Champion (billed with his dance partner as "Gower & Jeane").

Hellzapoppin 1938
46th Street Theatre [Richard Rodgers] ★ 1,404 performances

"A helter-skelter assembly of low-comedy gags to an ear-splitting sound accompaniment," said Brooks Atkinson of this scream-lined revue that was Broadway's longest-running musical until surpassed by *Oklahoma!* "If you can imagine a demented vaudeville brawl without the Marx Brothers, *Hellzapoppin* is it." Illustrator Fred Morgan captures many of the zany variety acts that comprised the show.

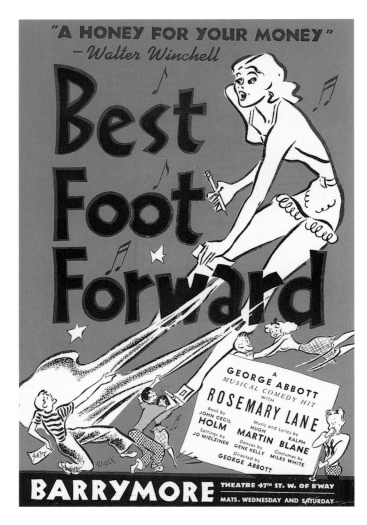

Carmen Jones 1943
Broadway Theatre ★ 502 performances
Post-Broadway tour (Boston)

The runaway success of *Oklahoma!* enabled lyricist-librettist Oscar Hammerstein to find backing for his dazzling retelling of Bizet's *Carmen.* Transported to a World War II–era parachute factory in the Deep South, the unlikely *Carmen Jones* proved an artistic and financial hit.

Best Foot Forward 1941
Ethel Barrymore Theatre ★ 326 performances

"Blessedly young, wonderfully expert and contagiously high-spirited," said the *World-Telegram.* "Youth and pleasure meet to provide one of those rejuvenating evenings at which George Abbott is a master." Marx's artwork handily captures the high spirits of this joyous college musical.

Something for the Boys 1943
Alvin Theatre [Neil Simon] ★ 422 performances

"Men growing old ungracefully wept to see what they never hoped to see again—the staging of a musical show as glamorous, kinetic, balanced and seductive as the still lamented Ziegfeld in his hey-day used to stage them," said the *World-Telegram.* Ethel Merman was the star, but the illustration indicates just what the boys were looking for.

Michael Todd's Mexican Hayride
Winter Garden, New York City

Mexican Hayride 1944
Winter Garden Theatre ★ 481 performances

"Magnificent, stupendous, terrific, colossal," said the *Mirror*, "a smash hit." While Cole Porter wrote the score and Bobby Clark headlined, all eyes were on the ladies, as evidenced by this specially commissioned Vargas girl.

"A SMASH HIT!" —WALTER WINCHELL

CHARLES LEDERER presents

WILLIAM JOHNSON ★ ELAINE MALBIN

in EDWIN LESTER'S production of

A MUSICAL ARABIAN NIGHT

Kismet

with Music from ALEXANDER BORODIN
Musical Adaptation & Lyrics by ROBERT WRIGHT & GEORGE FORREST
Book by CHARLES LEDERER & LUTHER DAVIS
(Based on the play by EDWARD KNOBLOCK)
Orchestral & Choral Arrangements by ARTHUR KAY

with

JULIE WILSON

HENRY CALVIN   BEATRICE KRAFT

Directed by ALBERT MARRE
Dances & Musical Numbers Staged by JACK COLE
Settings & Costumes Designed by LEMUEL AYERS
Lighting by PEGGY CLARK
Musical Direction by CARMINE COPPOLA

"Lavish! Gay! Terrific!"
N.Y. Journal-American

"A GAY, BRIGHT AND BRILLIANT FARCE" RICHARD WATTS N.Y. HER. TRIB.

JOHN C. WILSON PRESENTS

CLIFTON WEBB ⋆ PEGGY WOOD ⋆ LEONORA CORBETT ⋆ MILDRED NATWICK

IN

BLITHE SPIRIT

AN IMPROBABLE FARCE BY

NOEL COWARD

STAGED BY Mr. WILSON ⋆ SETTING BY STEWART CHANEY

Kismet 1953
Ziegfeld Theatre ★ 583 performances
National tour (Los Angeles)

Mystery, sex, and music are the components of the artwork for this "musical Arabian night." With such a masterful Hirschfeld at hand, the producers used this art for the touring company even though it clearly depicts original cast star Alfred Drake.

Blithe Spirit 1941
Morosco Theatre ★ 657 performances

"A completely insane farce that is also uproarious," said Brooks Atkinson, "it hardly touches the stage as it rides a demented broomstick to hilarity." Constantin Alajálov took his cue from the séance that figures prominently in the action of Noël Coward's most successful Broadway offering.

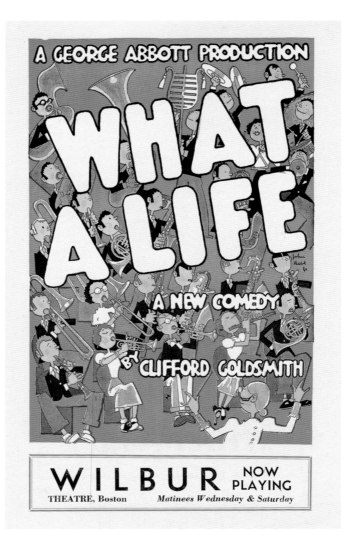

Russet Mantle 1936
Masque Theatre [John Golden] ★ 116 performances

"Literate and laughable, funny and profound," said the *World-Telegram* of this forgotten play, with "the most delightfully delirious dialogue to be heard on Broadway." Ludwig Bemelmans, of *Madeline* fame, provided the artwork.

What a Life 1938
Biltmore Theatre ★ 538 performances
National tour (Boston)

"A hurricane of laughs," said the *Mirror* of this George Abbott farce, which was spun off to become the radio and film series *Henry Aldrich.* "It should subject the town's funnybone to terrific punishment for a lengthy spell." The artwork came from John Held Jr., the magazine illustrator best known for his Roaring Twenties–era flappers.

THE 1939 PULITZER PRIZE PLAY

The Playwrights' Company

MAXWELL   S. N.   SIDNEY   ELMER   ROBERT E.
ANDERSON   BEHRMAN   HOWARD   RICE   SHERWOOD

PRESENT

RAYMOND MASSEY

IN ROBERT E. SHERWOOD'S *New Play*

"ABE LINCOLN IN ILLINOIS"

STAGED BY ELMER RICE
SETTINGS BY JO MIELZINER

PLYMOUTH THEATRE

West 45th St., New York City   *Mats. Wed. & Sat.*

Abe Lincoln in Illinois 1938
Plymouth Theatre ★ 472 performances

"It cannot and must not be missed by one who loves his country and his theatre," said the *World-Telegram*. Norman Rockwell's fanciful portrait combined the features of star Raymond Massey with those of the young Lincoln. Massey fashioned his makeup after Norman Rockwell's rendering.

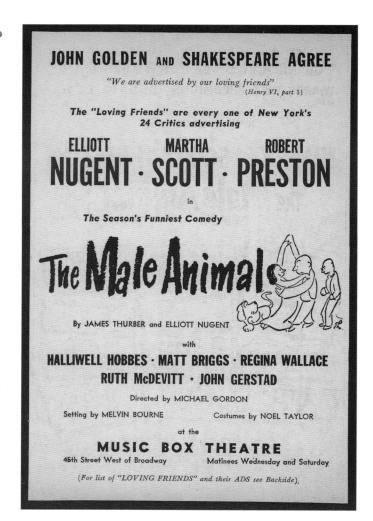

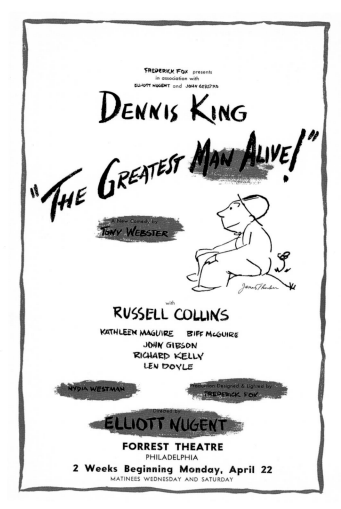

The Male Animal 1952
Music Box Theatre ★ 317 performances

This revival of James Thurber and Elliott Nugent's 1940 comedy about academic freedom outran the original, thanks in part to its enhanced topicality as Joe McCarthy was reaching the height of his power. Thurber's artwork directly illustrates the action, with the Thurberian professor glowering as his wife is romanced by the visiting football hero.

The Greatest Man Alive! 1957
Ethel Barrymore Theatre ★ 5 performances
Pre-Broadway tryout (Philadelphia), preliminary credits

This screwball farce about a suicidal old codger quickly expired, despite the presence of 1920s operetta star Dennis King. James Thurber provided the art for his college buddy and *Male Animal* collaborator, director-producer Elliott Nugent.

Under the Yum Yum Tree 1960
Henry Miller's Theatre ★ 173 performances

"Almost unbearable," said the *Post*. "For all its endeavors to be gay, witty and charming, it is remarkably lacking in all these qualities, achieving a kind of tasteless vulgarity." Peter Arno's maiden, nevertheless, is all innocence.

Anniversary Waltz 1954
Broadhurst Theatre ★ 615 performances
Post-Broadway tour (Chicago)

A forgettable comedy about premarital sex and mothers-in-law, but oh, what an arresting piece of art from Charles Addams, the master of the macabre!

The Best Man 1960
Morosco Theatre ★ 520 performances
Post-Broadway tour (St. Louis)

"A drama of size, written skillfully about people who bear a quaint resemblance
to living characters," said the *Journal-American.* "Performed with brilliance,
directed with taste and mounted in the style it deserves." One of the plot points
deals with a presidential candidate seeking the endorsement of the head of
the Women's Committee, comically rendered by Tomi Ungerer.

The Conquering Hero 1961
ANTA Theatre [Virginia] ★ 8 performances
Pre-Broadway tryout (Washington), preliminary credits

A musical so troubled that director-choreographer Bob Fosse—who thought it
up in the first place—was axed out-of-town, along with his "Guadalcanal Ballet."
William Steig's artwork shows the hero hoisted with his own flagpole, as it were.
An oft-misattributed quote, from librettist Larry Gelbart: "If Hitler's alive, I hope
he's out of town with a musical."

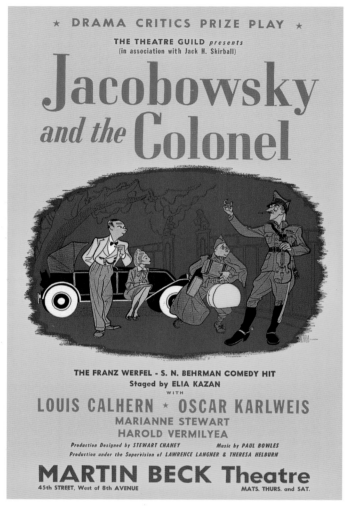

The Eve of St. Mark 1942
Cort Theatre ★ 306 performances

"*The Eve of St. Mark* brings the war home as it needs to be brought home," said the *World-Telegram*. "It is hard to see how any American could remain unaffected in its presence." This uncredited artwork appears to be by Norman Rockwell, who did the *Abe Lincoln in Illinois* artwork for the same producers.

Jacobowsky and the Colonel 1944
Martin Beck Theatre [Al Hirschfeld] ★ 417 performances

This comedy-drama mixed "sense, wit and poetry in a memorable theatrical reflection of the war," said the *Herald Tribune*, further noting that "Elia Kazan is rapidly becoming a great director." Al Hirschfeld provided color artwork for the occasion.

No Time for Sergeants 1955
Alvin Theatre [Neil Simon] ★ 796 performances
Pre-Broadway tryout (New Haven)

"Laughter like thunder will shake the Alvin Theatre for a long time to come," said the *World-Telegram* about this comedy, which made a star of Andy Griffith. "People walked out holding their sides, still gasping." The grand scenic effects from designer Peter Larkin included an onstage parachute drop, reflected in this artwork by B. Tobey.

Call Me Mister 1946
National Theatre [Nederlander] ★ 734 performances

This revue—written, staffed, and performed by ex-servicemen and women—was "a boisterous romp," said the *Herald Tribune*, "captivating, fresh, and vigorous." The artwork by *Yank* magazine cartoonist Sgt. Ralph Stein captures the joy of an ex-GI trading in his uniform for civilian garb.

The Best House in Naples 1956
Lyceum Theatre ★ 3 performances
Pre-Broadway tryout (Philadelphia), preliminary credits

The source material for this quick failure—the 1950 Italian play *Filumena Marturano*—served as the basis for the 1964 Marcello Mastroianni–Sophia Loren film *Marriage Italian-Style*. The art, depicting Academy Award–nominee Katy Jurado (of *High Noon*), indicates just what sort of house this was.

Anna Lucasta 1944
Mansfield Theatre [Brooks Atkinson] ★ 957 performances
Post-Broadway tour (Boston)

This *Anna Christie*-like tale of a prostitute turned good, intended as a Polish family drama, was initially produced by the American Negro Theatre in Harlem. The vibrant acting resulted in a quick transfer to Broadway, where it was a surprise wartime hit.

There's a Girl in My Soup 1967
Music Box Theatre ★ 322 performances
Pre-Broadway tryout (Boston)

Tomi Ungerer's cartoonish artwork helped fuel this undistinguished British sex farce—about "a TV epicure who accidentally falls in love with a delicious mini-skirted blonde with a far-out concept of mod morality"—for a successful ten-month run.

Irma La Douce 1960
Plymouth Theatre ★ 524 performances

Irma the sweet—"the girl who helps all Paris to relax, for just a thousand francs (including tax)"—towers over the city. "An eyebrow raiser drenched in sex, a zany carnival of song-and-dance," said the *Mirror*. "Wacky and exciting, and a real orb-popper when the saucy and sexy Elizabeth Seal is in the spotlight."

Look Back in Anger 1957
Lyceum Theatre ★ 407 performances

"The already-famous protest play of Britain's post-war generation is an absorbing and powerful drama, forceful and beautifully written, filled with stinging wit and almost ferocious scorn," said the *Post*. The *Times* refused to run the suggestive artwork.

Alfie! 1964
Morosco Theatre ★ 21 performances

"Puritans, perhaps, may tut-tut Alfie's winning way with women" the press agent promised about this poorly received British sex farce. *Alfie!* was nevertheless transformed into a 1966 film hit for Michael Caine, with a still-remembered title song by Burt Bacharach and Hal David. Tom Morrow provided the leering leading man.

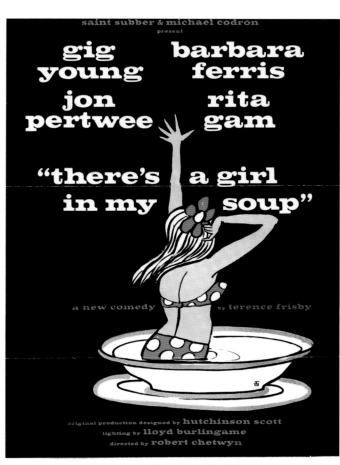

saint subber & michael codron present

gig young   barbara ferris
jon pertwee   rita gam

"there's a girl in my soup"

a new comedy by terence frisby

original production designed by hutchinson scott
lighting by lloyd burlingame
directed by robert chetwyn

COLONIAL THEATRE
BOSTON
3 WEEKS • MON. SEPT. 25 THRU SAT. OCT. 14
Opening Night Curtain at 8:00 P.M.   Evenings thereafter at 8:30 P.M.
Matinees Wed. at 2:00 P.M. and Sat. at 2:30 P.M.

"A SWEETHEART OF A MUSICAL"
— JOHN CHAPMAN, News

DAVID MERRICK
In association with DONALD ALBERY and H. M. TENNENT, LTD.
and by arrangement with Henry Hall
presents

ELIZABETH   KEITH
SEAL MICHELL
in the
PETER BROOK PRODUCTION of

IRMA LA DOUCE

A New Musical Comedy
with CLIVE REVILL
Music by MARGUERITE MONNOT
Original Book and Lyrics by ALEXANDRE BREFFORT
English Book and Lyrics by
JULIAN MORE, DAVID HENEKER and MONTY NORMAN
Dances and Musical Numbers staged by ONNA WHITE
Settings and Costumes by ROLF GERARD
Orchestrations by ANDRE POPP   Vocal Arrangements by BERT WALLER
Additional Arrangements & Orchestrations by ROBERT GINZLER
Musical Direction by STANLEY LEBOWSKY
Directed by PETER BROOK
ELIZABETH SEAL — 1961 Tony Award Winner

PLYMOUTH THEATRE
236 WEST 45th STREET, N. Y. C. 36
SEATS NOW — MAIL ORDERS ACCEPTED

DAVID MERRICK
presents

MARY URE
KENNETH HAIGH
LOOK BACK IN ANGER

a new play by
JOHN OSBORNE
with
ALAN BATES   VIVIENNE DRUMMOND
directed by
TONY RICHARDSON
OPENING ON BROADWAY OCTOBER 1
(See reverse side for convenient mail order form)
LYCEUM THEATRE 45th St. E. of B'way

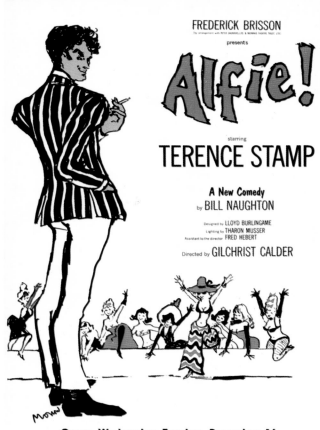

FREDERICK BRISSON
(by arrangement with PETER SAUNDERS LTD. & MEMORIAL THEATRE TRUST LTD.)
presents

Alfie!
starring
TERENCE STAMP

A New Comedy
by BILL NAUGHTON
Designed by LLOYD BURLINGAME
Lighting by THARON MUSSER
Assistant to the director FRED HEBERT
Directed by GILCHRIST CALDER

Opens Wednesday Evening, December 16
MOROSCO THEATRE
45th STREET WEST OF BROADWAY
Evenings at 8:30 -:- Matinees Wednesday at 2:00; Saturday at 2:30

The Night Circus 1958
Golden Theatre ★ 7 performances
Pre-Broadway tryout (Philadelphia)

This quick failure about a stormy interclass romance reunited the playwright,
director, producer, and star of the 1955 hit *A Hatful of Rain*. "Sordid and endless,"
said Brooks Atkinson. "If it proves anything, it proves that once a playwright
gets into a bar he should stay there."

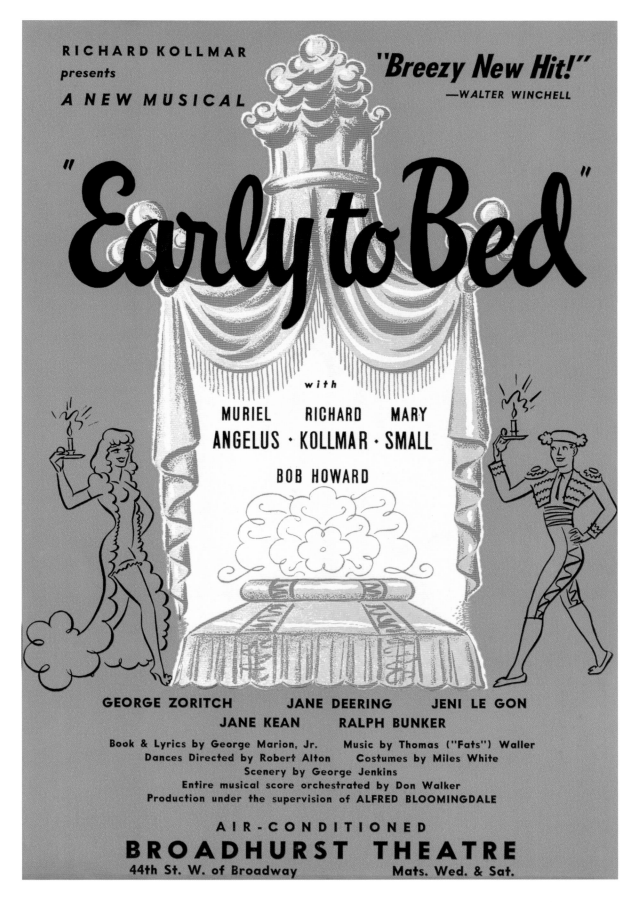

Early to Bed 1943
Broadhurst Theatre ★ 380 performances

This "fairy tale for grownups," about a house of ill repute mistaken for a finishing school, "is a bordello's night dream," said the *Daily News*. It was the first and only Broadway hit for Thomas "Fats" Waller, who died midway through the run.

"Broadway has found a triumph in 'EQUUS'"
– Clive Barnes. N.Y. Times

Kermit Bloomgarden and Doris Cole Abrahams
in association with Frank Milton present

EQUUS

By
Peter Shaffer

Starring
Douglas Campbell
Keith McDermott

Directed by
John Dexter

1975's Most Acclaimed Play!
New York Drama Critics Award
New York Outer Critics Award
Drama Desk Award
Tony Award
Tony and Drama Desk/Best Director

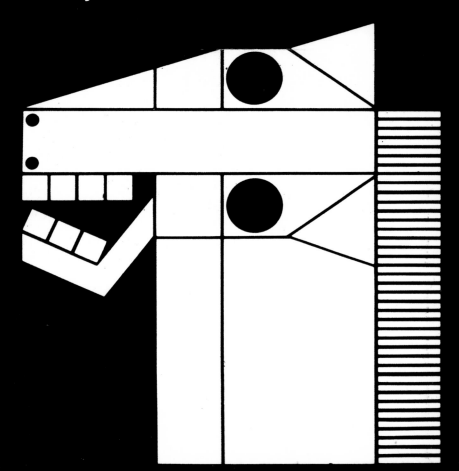

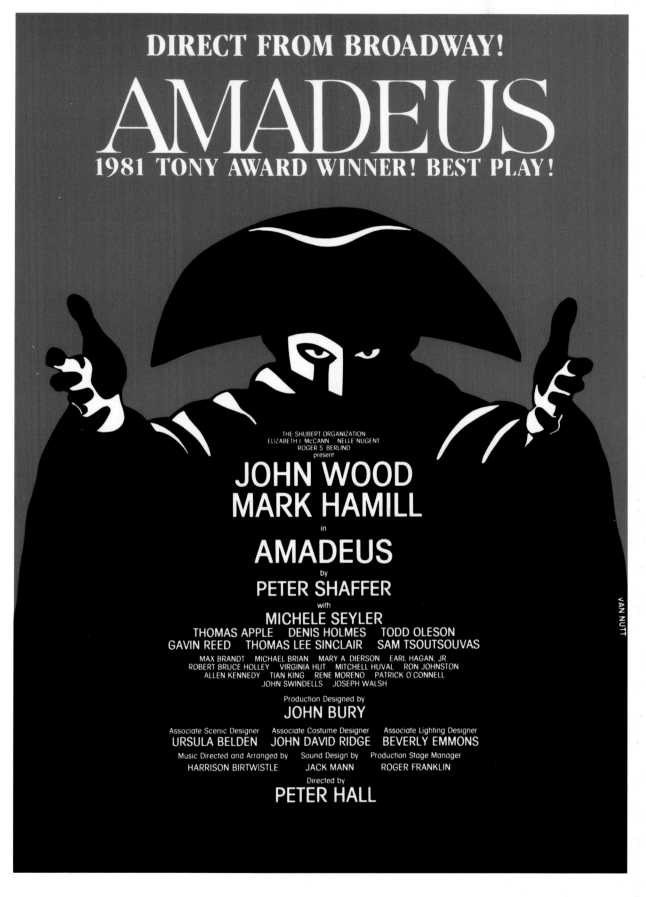

DIRECT FROM BROADWAY!

AMADEUS

1981 TONY AWARD WINNER! BEST PLAY!

THE SHUBERT ORGANIZATION
ELIZABETH I. McCANN   NELLE NUGENT
ROGER S. BERLIND
present

JOHN WOOD
MARK HAMILL

in

AMADEUS

by

PETER SHAFFER

with

MICHELE SEYLER

THOMAS APPLE   DENIS HOLMES   TODD OLESON
GAVIN REED   THOMAS LEE SINCLAIR   SAM TSOUTSOUVAS

MAX BRANDT   MICHAEL BRIAN   MARY A. DIERSON   EARL HAGAN, JR.
ROBERT BRUCE HOLLEY   VIRGINIA HUT   MITCHELL HUVAL   RON JOHNSTON
ALLEN KENNEDY   TIAN KING   RENE MORENO   PATRICK O'CONNELL
JOHN SWINDELLS   JOSEPH WALSH

Production Designed by
JOHN BURY

Associate Scenic Designer   Associate Costume Designer   Associate Lighting Designer
URSULA BELDEN   **JOHN DAVID RIDGE**   **BEVERLY EMMONS**

Music Directed and Arranged by   Sound Design by   Production Stage Manager
HARRISON BIRTWISTLE   **JACK MANN**   **ROGER FRANKLIN**

Directed by
PETER HALL

VAN NUTT

Equus 1974
Plymouth Theatre ★ 1,209 performances
National tour (Baltimore)

Peter Shaffer's psychological drama about a young psychiatric
patient who has unaccountably blinded six horses, had one of
the most striking Broadway poster designs ever. Gilbert Lesser's
enigmatic artwork represents a blind horse, patterned on a
chess piece.

Amadeus 1980
Broadhurst Theatre ★ 1,181 performances
National tour (Baltimore)

Peter Shaffer's fantastical drama, about Mozart as seen through
the eyes of the all-but-forgotten composer Antonio Salieri,
was a major hit in London, the United States, and on the
screen. Robert Van Nutt's artwork corresponds to Salieri's
encounter with Mozart in the climactic scene.

1776

America's
Award Winning
Musical

NATIONAL THEATRE

WASHINGTON, D. C. 20004

MAY 23 *thru* JULY 8

1776 1969
46th Street Theatre [Richard Rodgers] ★ 1,217 performances
National tour (Washington)

"A most striking, most gripping musical," said Clive Barnes
about this patriotic hit, "a musical with style, humanity, wit
and passion." Fay Gage's artwork represents a comical eaglet
being born, as in the song "The Egg."

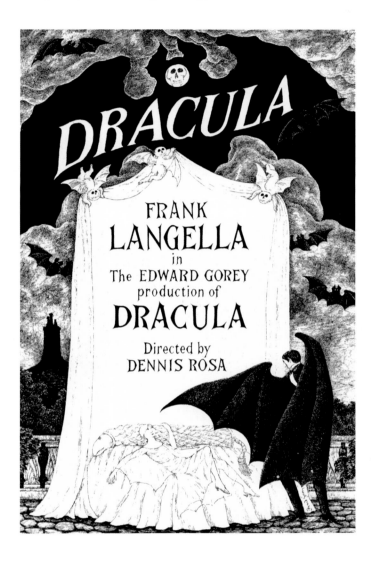

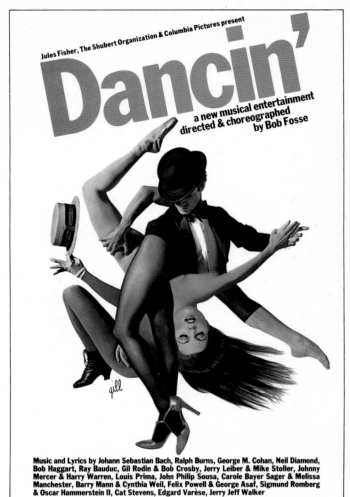

Dracula 1977
Martin Beck Theatre [Al Hirschfeld] ★ 925 performances
Pre-Broadway tryout (Boston)

The macabre designs of Edward Gorey and a tongue-in-cheek
performance by Frank Langella turned this revival of the 1925
play into a surprise hit.

Dancin' 1978
Broadhurst Theatre ★ 1,774 performances

Bob Fosse's dance revue was heralded by Bob Gill's striking
art, featuring five legs, four arms, and two hats. All dancin',
all Fosse.

leland hayward
presents a new comedy
by george axelrod

lauren bacall

"goodbye charlie"

sydney chaplin

and

cara williams

bert thorn

directed by the author
production designed by oliver smith
lighting by peggy clark
miss bacall's clothes by mainbocher
other clothes by florence klotz

FORD'S THEATRE
BALTIMORE
1 Week Only—Mon., Nov. 23 thru Sat., Nov. 28
Matinees Wednesday and Saturday

Goodbye Charlie 1959
Lyceum Theatre ★ 109 performances
Pre-Broadway tryout (Baltimore), preliminary credits

Brooks Atkinson found this lame sex farce about a lecher reincarnated as a lady
"inherently hopeless," adding that "since Lauren Bacall plays the part like a cross
between a female impersonator and Tallulah Bankhead, it is an amusing novelty
for a few moments." Still, it had striking artwork by Marcel Vertès.

Oh, Captain! 1958
Alvin Theatre [Neil Simon] ★ 192 performances

"Perhaps they should try making Broadway musicals out of bad movies," said
Walter Kerr about this adaptation of *The Captain's Paradise*. "They're still
having trouble making them out of good ones." Tom Morrow's delicious artwork
was censored in newspaper ads, with a filmy chemise drawn in under the apron.

Diana Rigg
Robert Helpmann   John Reardon
Martin Vidnovic   Marta Eggerth
in
Colette   A Musical

Book and Lyrics by
Tom Jones
Music by
Harvey Schmidt
Choreography by
Carl Jablonski
Entire Production Staged and Directed by
Dennis Rosa

HILARY KNIGHT 1982

Colette 1982
Closed out-of-town
Pre-Broadway tryout (Seattle)

Diana Rigg made her American musical comedy debut in this biography of
the famous French author. Despite some ravishing songs by Harvey Schmidt
and Tom Jones, the show never made it out of Seattle. Illustrator Hilary Knight
provided one of his typically stunning designs.

Allah Be Praised! 1944

Adelphi Theatre [George Abbott] ★ 20 performances

This "exotic and exciting" musical comedy mess produced by department-store heir Alfred Bloomingdale had music by Don Walker, "a harem-ful of delightful eyefuls," and Marcel Vertès's exquisitely artistic poster art.

Index

The plays and musicals represented are indexed below. Also included are the artists (where known) and some — but by no means all — of the creators, performers, and other key people involved.